Living Faiths

Buddhism
Teacher Guide

Mark Constance
Series Editor: Janet Dyson
Consultant: Robert Bowie

OXFORD
UNIVERSITY PRESS

Contents

Scheme of Work

This table shows links to themes in RE across the six faiths in the *Living Faiths* series, so that you can easily navigate through the series and teach by religion or by theme. The themes are organized alphabetically under the two headings, **Beliefs** and **Moral and Ethical Issues**.

	Buddhism	Christianity	Hinduism	Islam	Judaism	Sikhism
Beliefs						
Faith origins	Overview, 1.1	Overview	Overview, 2.1	Overview	Overview	Overview
Festivals / Celebrations	2.5, 2.6	3.5, 5.2	3.2, 3.3		2.6, 3.4, 3.5, 3.7	2.6, 3.4, 3.5
Food	5.4		4.4, 4.5	3.3, 3.5	3.2	3.6, 3.7
God / Divine		1.1, 1.2, 1.3, 1.4	1.1, 1.2, 4.6	1.2	1.1, 1.3	1.1, 1.2
Key teachings	1.3, 1.4, 2.3, 2.4, 3.4	1.3, 1.6, 2.2, 4.4, 4.7	1.3, 1.4, 1.6, 3.1, 3.4, 3.5, 4.1	1.1, 1.3, 1.5, 3.1, 3.2, 3.3, 3.4	1.2, 1.4, 1.5, 2.2, 2.5	1.3, 1.4
Life after death	1.6, 2.6	2.5, 2.6	1.3	4.1, 4.2	4.2, 4.3	1.4
Places of worship	2.7	2.5, 3.2	2.5	2.5, 3.4	3.3	3.3
Religious leaders	4.3, 5.5, 5.6	2.3	1.5, 2.4, 2.5, 3.1, 4.2	2.2, 2.3	1.5, 2.7	2.1, 2.2, 2.3, 2.4
Religious symbols / Dress	1.5, 3.3	3.1	2.1	3.6	3.6	3.1, 3.2
Sacred texts	2.1, 2.2	2.1, 2.2	2.2, 2.3	2.1, 2.4	2.1, 2.2, 2.3, 2.4	2.5
Worship	3.1, 3.2, 3.3, 3.5	1.5, 2.4, 3.2, 3.3, 3.4	3.2, 3.4, 3.6	1.3, 1.5, 3.1, 3.2, 3.3, 3.4	3.1, 3.3	3.3
Moral and Ethical Issues						
Environment / Animal rights	5.4	5.4	4.4, 4.6, 4.7	4.5	4.6	4.2
Evil and suffering	1.3, 1.4	4.3, 4.5	4.2, 4.3	4.3, 4.4	4.5	5.2
Fair trade	4.4	5.5	5.5			
Gender and equality / Role of women	5.2		1.5, 5.4	3.6, 5.2	5.3	5.4
Interfaith	4.3	5.6	5.6	2.2, 5.6	5.5	5.6
Medical ethics	3.6	4.2	4.2	5.4	4.1	4.4, 4.5
Relationships / Marriage / Family	5.2	5.2, 5.3	3.3, 5.3	5.2, 5.3	5.1, 5.2	4.6
Science and religion	4.5	4.1		4.6, 5.4		4.3
Secular and atheist worldviews	4.5		1.1, 1.6	5.5	4.4, 5.5	4.3
War and peace	4.2, 5.5, 5.6	4.5, 4.6	3.1, 4.2, 5.5	4.3	5.5	5.2, 5.5
Wealth / Poverty / Charity	5.3	5.1, 5.6	3.1, 5.1	3.2	5.4	3.6, 3.8, 4.1

Introduction to *Living Faiths*

 ## How we live now

Living Faiths draws on the rich heritage of culture and diversity in twenty-first century Britain. The series focuses on case studies (shown through film and print) of young people and their families in the UK who describe how their faith affects the way they live and the moral and ethical decisions they make. The emphasis is on the personal significance of religious faith, exploring the question: What does it *mean* to be a Buddhist, Christian, Hindu, Jew, Muslim or Sikh?

This approach allows students to experience the subject fully and see its relevance to their own lives. Engagement with the case study families creates awareness of diversity, encouraging respect and enhancing social awareness. Hearing and seeing young people sharing their faith and aspects of their daily lives helps students clarify their own perspectives and reflect on their experiences, build their sense of identity and belonging, challenge prejudices and provide the knowledge and understanding to enable them to flourish in their communities.

 ## Flexible and adaptable

Living Faiths is a series of six books, teacher guides and online resources covering Buddhism, Christianity, Hinduism, Islam, Judaism, and Sikhism. The series is designed to allow teachers the flexibility to teach by faiths or by themes, and the Scheme of Work (on page 3) provides guidance at a glance on how to teach by themes. Through structured questioning and activities, students are encouraged to make links as they learn about a range of faiths and secular world views. They are expected to identify similarities and differences within faiths, and the *Teacher Guide* further provides suggestions on how to compare and contrast between faiths. There is a strong emphasis on sources including sacred texts, film interviews, audio and music

to give students access to the lived experience of the case study families and learn what their faith means in practice.

 ## Pedagogy

The series takes a mixed pedagogical approach inspired by the important ethnographic work that has been developed in RE in recent years. Throughout the series students are introduced to the study of faith as it is practised by believers today. The enquiry-driven focus enables them to engage with the voices and personalities of faith, getting beyond generalizations and over-simplifications, to enter into dialogue with people about their faith. Through this dialogue with living faith students will be encouraged to reflect on the experiences and beliefs of others and also on their own experiences of faith, belief and what really matters in life.

The *Living Faiths* series has been designed to engage, interest and challenge students. Each unit has an intriguing title, often a question, to capture the interest of students as soon as the lesson begins. The 'starter' activities get students thinking and discussing, drawing on their prior learning or their personal experiences as ways into the main lesson focus.

 ## Questioning

Questioning is fundamental to good teaching and learning. Higher order questions enable students to tackle issues at a deep level and extend their thinking, develop independence in the way they learn and think and come to a fuller understanding of an idea because they have tried to explain it themselves. Bloom's Taxonomy (1956), is a useful tool for planning sequences of different types of questions of increasing difficulty to promote higher order thinking. Many of the activities are designed for pair and group discussion or for independent and small group research to promote student participation. Through the activities students will develop the ability to speculate, to raise their own questions and seek answers for themselves.

Reflection

Do you think people in Britain live sheltered lives in any way? What things do you think they are sheltered from?

Activities

1. Siddattha's father wanted him to be a great ruler rather than a great religious leader. Why do you think some people place more importance on being a leader in the material world than being a spiritual leader? Discuss with a partner.

2. Which is better, a fake world where nothing bad happens or a real world where there is the possibility of bad things happening? Write a speech explaining your view or a modern story that shows somebody trapped in a fake world.

3. What stories and films, such as *The Matrix*, can you think of that remind you of the story so far? Explain your choice.

The activities are colour coded to identify three modes of thinking that are particularly valuable in the study of religion, philosophy and the broad area of social sciences.

Students are encouraged to:

- **Red: 'Think like a theologian'** these questions focus on understanding the nature of religious belief, its symbolism and spiritual significance; in the *Student Book* they are highlighted by a red question number

- **Blue: 'Think like a philosopher'** these questions focus on analysing and debating big ideas such as truth and reality; in the *Student Book* they are highlighted by a blue question number

- **Green: 'Think like a social scientist'** these questions focus on exploring and analysing why people do what they do and how belief affects action; in the *Student Book* they are highlighted by a green question number

 ### Reflection

Reflection helps students to deepen their thinking and apply their learning about the religious beliefs and practices of others. It encourages them to explore their own beliefs in the light of what they learn, whether they are religious or not, and how they impact on personal ethics.

Thinking skills

In RE students are expected to think in increasing depth about complex issues to do with faith, beliefs, ideas and motivation. Philosophical enquiry-based approaches such as mind-mapping help students to think creatively, analytically and critically; to listen to, evaluate and respond to the views and ideas of others; to give reasons for their opinions, make connections and hypothesize; to give both sides of an argument, evaluate and draw conclusions.

Assessment

At the end of each unit there is a final assessment task which draws together students' learning.

Assessment for learning strategies are built into every unit:

- Learning objectives for each unit are written in student-friendly language and shared with students
- Students know what standards and levels they are aiming for
- Self- and peer-assessment opportunities are supported by 'I can' statements
- **AT1 Learning *about* religion** is assessed using auto-marked tests to help save you time setting questions and marking
- **AT2 Learning *from* religion** is assessed with step-by-step tasks and support materials. These use effective assessment for learning strategies to help students recognize next steps and improve performance.

We hope that you will enjoy using this series to bring real families of faith into the classroom, and to introduce students to the liveliness and relevance of religious education.

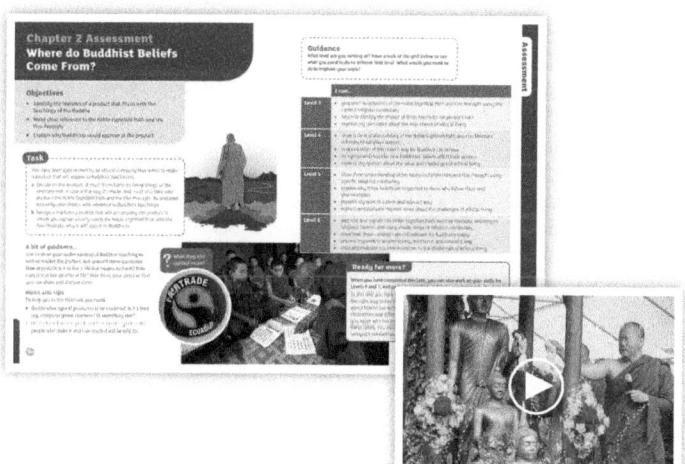

Janet Dyson
(Series Editor)

Robert Bowie
(Series Consultant)

About this Series

Living Faiths Buddhism is one of six Religious Education Student Books covering the following major faiths: Buddhism, Christianity, Hinduism, Islam, Judaism, and Sikhism. This series fully integrates real-life film clips and other exciting multimedia resources on *Kerboodle* with the *Student Books* and *Teacher Guides*, so your lessons can be delivered easily and seamlessly.

The series components

The series consist of:

For students

- Six *Student Books* (and/or six *Kerboodle Books*)
- Six *Kerboodle* Lessons, Resources and Assessments.

For teachers

- Six *Teacher Guides*
- Six *Kerboodle* Lessons, Resources and Assessments (includes teacher access to the accompanying *Kerboodle Book*).

Student Book

The *Living Faiths Buddhism Student Book* uses **real-life case studies** to encourage students to ask questions, actively engage with **moral** and **ethical** issues, and reflect on the relevance of RE.

> Starter activities spark your students' interest in new topics

> The 'Reflection' feature helps your students to consider beliefs and practices of others, and how they link to their own lives and beliefs

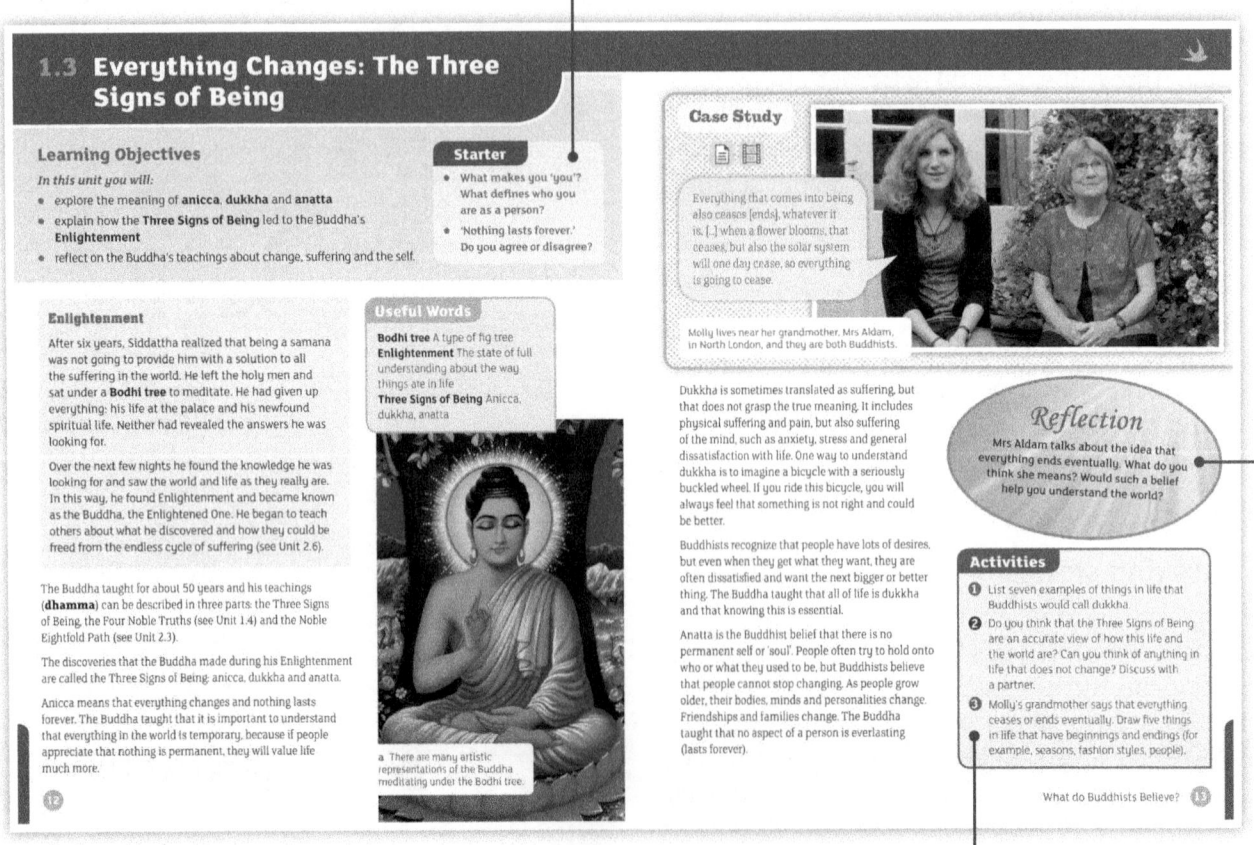

Buddhism Student Book

> Colour-coded activities develop varied skills and are structured to encourage progression and allow differentiation

Case studies provide first-hand experience of real Buddhist families talking about their faith

Buddhism Student Book

There is an assessment spread for every chapter in the *Student Book* to help students determine what level they are aiming for and make progress

Extensions tasks within assessments challenge more able students

Case studies are linked directly to films on *Kerboodle* and are marked with film icons on each page

Authors

Experienced RE Consultant **Janet Dyson** and well-known author and PGCE tutor **Robert Bowie** lead the author **Mark Constance**, who is an experienced RE teacher.

Buddhism Kerboodle

Using this Book

Teacher Guide

The ***Living Faiths Buddhism Teacher Guide*** aims to save you time and effort. It provides **full support** and guidance for the *Buddhism Student Book*, including **practical tasks** and **creative suggestions** for incorporating differentiation into your teaching.

What it provides

For each chapter of the student book, this book provides:

- a chapter overview
- help at a glance for each unit
- further suggestions for class and homework
- an assessment overview.

It also has a **Glossary** at the back, covering the RE terms students will meet.

Please turn to the **Contents List** on page 2 to see how this book is structured. While the Living Faiths series is organized by religion, a **Scheme of Work** on page 3 is also provided to help you teach RE **by themes**.

Find out more about the four main components below.

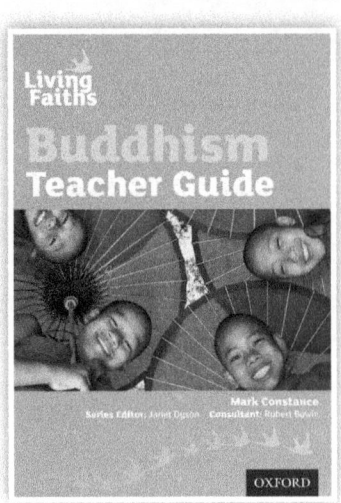

The chapter overview

This is your introduction to the corresponding *Student Book* chapter.

Shows how the *Student Book* chapter relates to the KS3 RE Programme of Study (non-statutory)

Reminds you that some lessons, including starters and plenaries, will need resources prepared in advance

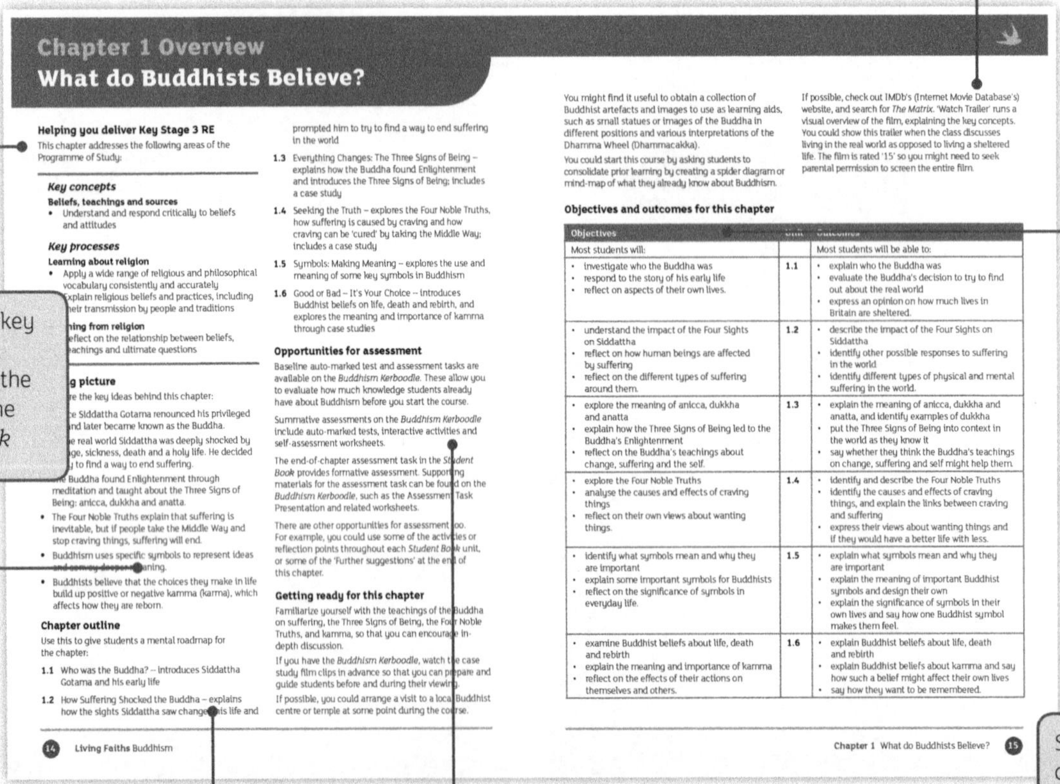

Chapter 1 Overview
What do Buddhists Believe?

Helping you deliver Key Stage 3 RE

This chapter addresses the following areas of the Programme of Study:

Key concepts

Beliefs, teachings and sources

- Understand and respond critically to beliefs and attitudes

Key processes

Learning about religion

- Apply a wide range of religious and philosophical vocabulary consistently and accurately
- xplain religious beliefs and practices, including eir transmission by people and traditions

ing from religion

eflect on the relationship between beliefs, achings and ultimate questions

g picture

e the key ideas behind this chapter:

e Siddattha Gotama renounced his privileged nd later became known as the Buddha.

e real world Siddattha was deeply shocked by ge, sickness, death and a holy life. He decided to find a way to end suffering.

Buddha found Enlightenment through meditation and taught about the Three Signs of Being: anicca, dukkha and anatta.

- The Four Noble Truths explain that suffering is inevitable, but if people take the Middle Way and stop craving things, suffering will end.
- Buddhism uses specific symbols to represent ideas aning.
- Buddhists believe that the choices they make in life build up positive or negative kamma (karma), which affects how they are reborn.

Chapter outline

Use this to give students a mental roadmap for the chapter:

1.1 Who was the Buddha? – introduces Siddattha Gotama and his early life

1.2 How Suffering Shocked the Buddha – explains how the sights Siddattha saw change is life and prompted him to try to find a way to end suffering in the world

1.3 Everything Changes: The Three Signs of Being – explains how the Buddha found Enlightenment and introduces the Three Signs of Being; includes a case study

1.4 Seeking the Truth – explores the Four Noble Truths, how suffering is caused by craving and how craving can be 'cured' by taking the Middle Way; includes a case study

1.5 Symbols: Making Meaning – explores the use and meaning of some key symbols in Buddhism

1.6 Good or Bad – It's Your Choice – introduces Buddhist beliefs on life, death and rebirth, and explores the meaning and importance of kamma through case studies

Opportunities for assessment

Baseline auto-marked test and assessment tasks are available on the *Buddhism Kerboodle*. These allow you to evaluate how much knowledge students already have about Buddhism before you start the course.

Summative assessments on the *Buddhism Kerboodle* include auto-marked tests, interactive activities and self-assessment worksheets.

The end-of-chapter assessment task in the *Student Book* provides formative assessment. Supporting materials for the assessment task can be found on the *Buddhism Kerboodle*, such as the Assessment Task Presentation and related worksheets.

There are other opportunities for assessment too. For example, you could use some of the activities or reflection points throughout each *Student Book* unit, or some of the 'Further suggestions' at the end of this chapter.

Getting ready for this chapter

Familiarize yourself with the teachings of the Buddha on suffering, the Three Signs of Being, the Four Noble Truths, and kamma, so that you can encourage in-depth discussion.

If you have the *Buddhism Kerboodle*, watch the case study film clips in advance so that you can prepare and guide students before and during their viewing.

If possible, you could arrange a visit to a local Buddhist centre or temple at some point during the course.

You might find it useful to obtain a collection of Buddhist artefacts and images to use as learning aids, such as small statues or images of the Buddha in different positions and various interpretations of the Dharmma Wheel (Dhammacakka).

You could start this course by asking students to consolidate prior learning by creating a spider diagram or mind-map of what they already know about Buddhism.

If possible, check out IMDb's (Internet Movie Database's) website, and search for *The Matrix*. 'Watch Trailer' runs a visual overview of the film, explaining the key concepts. You could show this trailer when the class discusses living in the real world as opposed to living a sheltered life. The film is rated '15' so you might need to seek parental permission to screen the entire film.

Objectives and outcomes for this chapter

Objectives		
Most students will:		Most students will be able to:
• investigate who the Buddha was • respond to the story of his early life • reflect on aspects of their own lives.	1.1	• explain who the Buddha was • evaluate the Buddha's decision to try to find out about the real world • express an opinion on how much lives in Britain are sheltered.
• understand the impact of the Four Sights on Siddattha • reflect on how human beings are affected by suffering • reflect on the different types of suffering around them.	1.2	• describe the impact of the Four Sights on Siddattha • identify other possible responses to suffering in the world • identify different types of physical and mental suffering in the world.
• explore the meaning of anicca, dukkha and anatta • explain how the Three Signs of Being led to the Buddha's Enlightenment • reflect on the Buddha's teachings about change, suffering and the self.	1.3	• explain the meaning of anicca, dukkha and anatta, and identify examples of dukkha • put the Three Signs of Being into context in the world as they know it • say whether they think the Buddha's teachings on change, suffering and self might help them.
• explore the Four Noble Truths • analyse the causes and effects of craving things • reflect on their own views about wanting things.	1.4	• identify and describe the Four Noble Truths • identify the causes and effects of craving things, and explain the links between craving and suffering • express their views about wanting things and if they would have a better life with less.
• identify what symbols mean and why they are important • explain some important symbols for Buddhists • reflect on the significance of symbols in everyday life.	1.5	• explain what symbols mean and why they are important • explain the meaning of important Buddhist symbols and design their own • explain the significance of symbols in their own lives and say how one Buddhist symbol makes them feel.
• examine Buddhist beliefs about life, death and rebirth • explain the meaning and importance of kamma • reflect on the effects of their actions on themselves and others.	1.6	• explain Buddhist beliefs about life, death and rebirth • explain Buddhist beliefs about kamma and say how such a belief might affect their own lives • say how they want to be remembered.

14 Living Faiths Buddhism

Chapter 1 What do Buddhists Believe? 15

Sets out the key ideas within, and behind, the chapter in the *Student Book*

Gives a brief summary of what's covered in the *Student Book* chapter. It will help you give students a road map for the chapter

Points you to the assessment material for the chapter (summative and formal assessments, and related resources)

Sets out the objectives and outcomes for the chapter, and the corresponding unit numbers

Help at a glance for each unit

These pages give comprehensive help for each unit of the *Student Book*.

Summarizes ideas covered in the unit, plus underlying ideas where appropriate

Starts with a brief walk through the unit, to show you how it develops

How Suffering Shocked the Buddha

The unit in brief
This unit explains what happened on Siddattha's journey outside the palace. It introduces the Four Sights and encourages students to empathize with their impact on Siddattha. It prompts students to reflect on the effects of suffering in the world.

Key ideas
- Siddattha saw Four Sights that had a huge impact on him: an old man, a sick man, a funeral, and a holy man
- He decided to lead a spiritual life to find a way to end the suffering in the world
- Suffering of one type or another is all around us in this world

Useful Words
Four Sights, samana

Skills practised
- Literacy: reading independently
- Empathy: understanding the impact of the Four Sights on Siddattha
- Thinking: considering what things shock us and the different types of suffering
- Reflection: considering how people are affected by suffering

Resources
- 1.2 Story Audio Clip: a reading of the story of the Four Sights that features in the *Student Book*
- 1.2 Letter Worksheet: students write a letter as if they were Siddattha, explaining their decision to leave or stay in the palace
- 1.2 Four Sights Interactive Activity: students identify the Four Sights that led to Siddattha's decision to become a samana
- 1.2 Lesson Player: a ready-to-go presentation with built-in resources and teacher notes
- 1 Image Gallery: a useful gallery of photos and illustrations from the chapter
- 1.2 Self-Assessment Sheet: students evaluate their learning against the lesson objectives

Ideas for starters
1. Ask students to write one thing that shocks them on a sticky note and stick it on the board. Share some of the ideas and develop a brief discussion on why and how some things shock and others do not.
2. Ask students to write ideas as above, but put all the notes in a box. Ask them to take notes out randomly and then form a continuum line, ordering how shocking they find the events on the sticky notes. Ask students to share their reasoning.

Activity guidance
- For Activity 2 in the *Student Book*, make sure students understand that they should use the different types of suffering mentioned in *Majjhima Nikaya* 56:11 to inform their mind-map.

Ideas for plenaries
1. Use the Reflection from the *Student Book*.
2. Ask students to write three sentences to explain what they have learned from this unit.
3. Ask students to prepare a short piece of writing starting with 'I do/do not think we can solve the problem of suffering in the world because…'.
4. Ask students to explain to a partner, in one minute, whether they think the Buddha was right about all life being suffering.

Further class and homework activities
1. Ask students to imagine that they are interviewing Siddattha after he saw the Four Sights. What five questions would they like to ask him about what he saw?
2. Ask students to write a shock newspaper report under the headline: 'Shock as Buddha reveals all life is suffering'.
3. You could use 1.2 Letter Worksheet on the *Buddhism Kerboodle* at the end of the lesson or as a homework. When they are finished they could 'send' their letter to a classmate.
4. 1.2 Four Sights Interactive Activity on the *Buddhism Kerboodle*.
5. Further suggestions on page 28 of this book.

Chapter 1 What do Buddhists Be…

Suggestions for starters

This section provides clarification and extra information for some activities in the *Student Book*

New terms introduced in the unit. See the glossary at the back of the book

A list of all the resources available on *Kerboodle* for the unit

Suggests plenaries for use throughout the lesson, not just at the end

Points you to related material on *Kerboodle*, including interactive activities, worksheets, homework ideas and assessment opportunities

Further suggestions for class and homework

These pages give a bank of further suggestions for class and homework.

They have been graded *, ** or *** according to level of difficulty.

These suggestions are addressed directly to students.

2.1 Read All About It!
1. Create a poster that shows all of the sources of authority in your life. *
2. 'We all need authority in our lives.' Do you agree with this statement? Explain why or why not. **

2.5 Let's Celebrate!
1. Find out more about how Wesak is celebrated around the world. Make notes about the customs that people in different countries have for celebrating it. **
2. 'Celebrating special events encourages people in their faith.' Do you think that this statement is

Suggestions are graded, but some are suitable for all levels, and differentiated by outcome

The assessment overview

This section introduces you to the end-of-chapter assessment task from the *Student Book*, and describes the support materials available for the chapter.

Assessment in the *Student Book*
You will find an assessment task at the end of every chapter that focuses on AT2. In this chapter, the task asks students to design a poster that explains the Four Noble Truths, using images and quotations.

In the *Student Book* (and on the supporting worksheets), you'll find guidance about levels of assessment that you can use to help your students understand what their work should include. You could ask them to use these criteria for self- or peer-assessment once they've completed the task.

Living Faiths Assessment
Student Book
- Assessment Task
- Levels Guidance

Kerboodle
- Auto-Marked Test
- Assessment Task Presentation
- Assessment Worksheets

The purpose of the end-of-chapter assessment task from the *Student Book* is summarized

You can see all the assessment materials available for the chapter at a glance

Kerboodle

Living Faiths Buddhism Kerboodle is packed full of guided support and ideas for running and creating effective lessons on Buddhism. It's intuitive to use, customizable, and can be accessed online.

It consists of:

- Buddhism Lessons, Resources and Assessments (includes teacher access to the accompanying *Kerboodle Book*)
- *Buddhism Kerboodle Book*.

Lessons, Resources and Assessment

Living Faiths Buddhism Kerboodle – Lessons, Resources and Assessment provides over one hundred lively built-in resources, including unique specially commissioned films of real Buddhist families practising their faiths, interactive activities, ready-to-go lesson presentations, and supported assessment tasks. You can even **adapt** many of these resources to suit you and your students' individual needs, and **upload** your existing resources so everything can be accessed from one location. Image collections and audio clips are also included to help bring RE to life in your classroom.

Lessons, Resources and Assessment provides:

- Resources
- Lessons
- Assessment and Markbook
- Teacher access to the *Kerboodle Book*.

Find out more about the four main components below.

Resources

Click on the **Resources tab** at the top of the screen to access the full list of *Living Faiths Buddhism* resources.

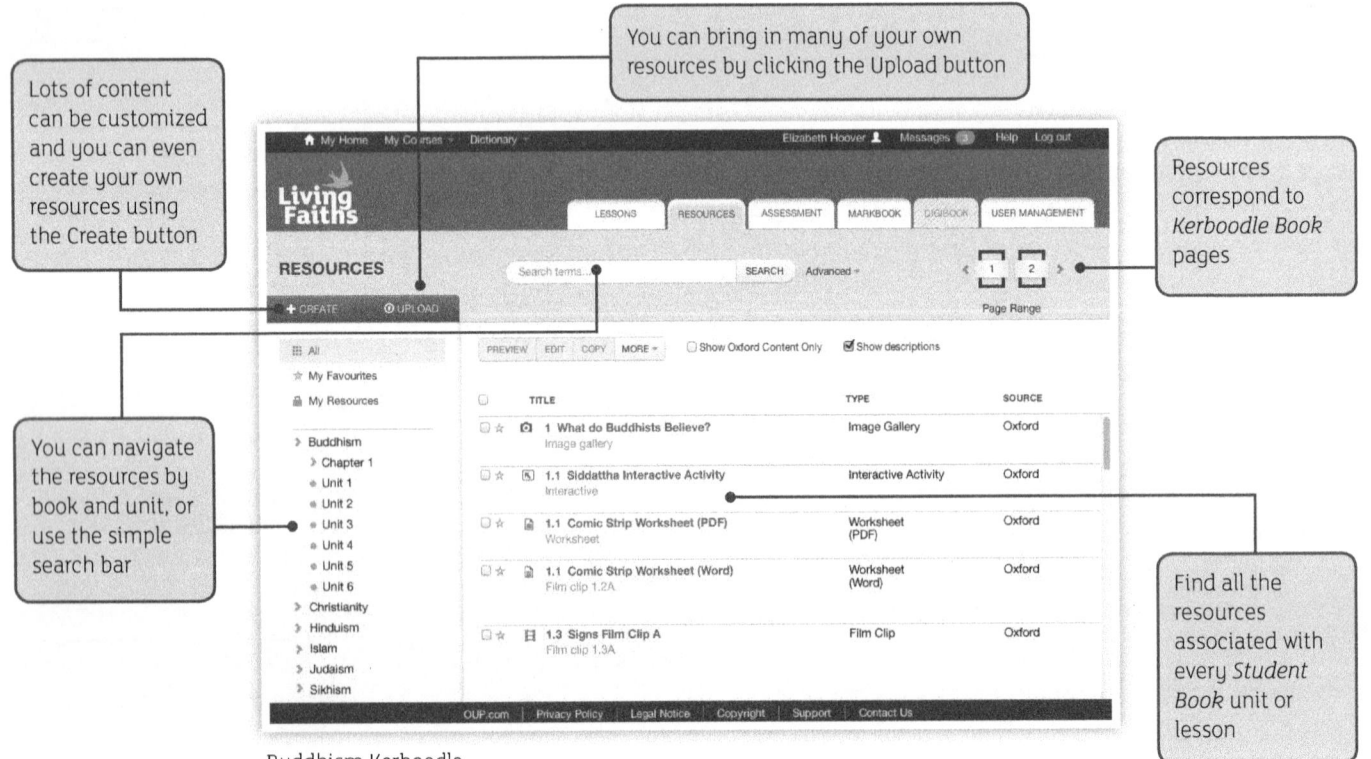

You can bring in many of your own resources by clicking the Upload button

Lots of content can be customized and you can even create your own resources using the Create button

Resources correspond to *Kerboodle Book* pages

You can navigate the resources by book and unit, or use the simple search bar

Find all the resources associated with every *Student Book* unit or lesson

Buddhism Kerboodle

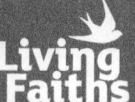

The Resources section has more than:

20 Film clips: Specially commissioned films help your students to actively engage with RE through watching real Buddhist families practise their faith and to explore the diversity within Buddhism.

10 Audio clips: Specially commissioned music and narrated sources help bring RE alive in your classroom.

70 Worksheets: Creative worksheets that help provide differentiation/extension material for each unit, and film worksheets to help students assess their own learning of the case study film clips and link ideas back to the *Student Book* unit. They are provided as PDFs, which you can print off and photocopy, and as Word files, which you can amend to suit your students' needs.

30 Interactive activities: Various types of activities are available for each unit as short main activities, plenaries or summative assessments. They can also be used for independent study. Most of these activities are auto-marked to help you save time marking.

80 Images: An image gallery with captions is provided for each chapter so you can easily enlarge any photo or artwork from the *Student Book* on screen and use it as a discussion starter, use them in your own worksheets, or give them to students to use in class or homework activities.

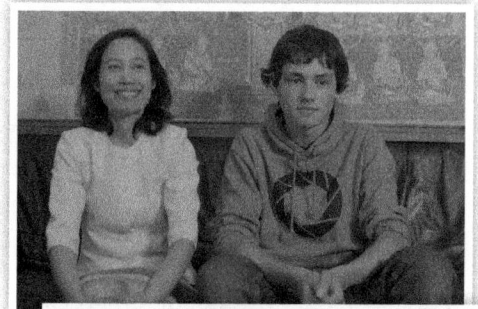

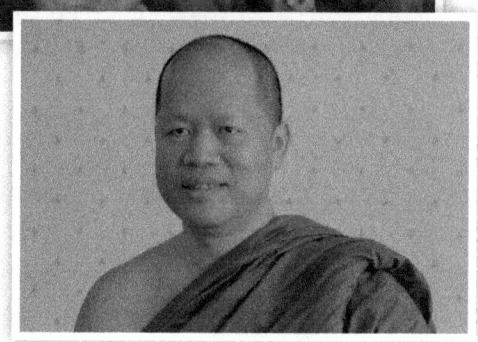

Kerboodle Resources are fully integrated with the *Student Book*:

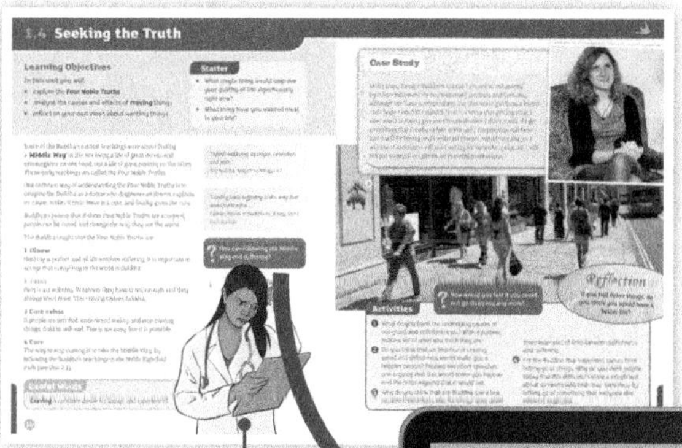

Buddhism
Student Book

Real Buddhist families are featured in the *Student Book* and you can find the specially commissioned films related to *Student Book* units on *Kerboodle*

Use the accompanying film worksheets to help your students consolidate what they have learnt

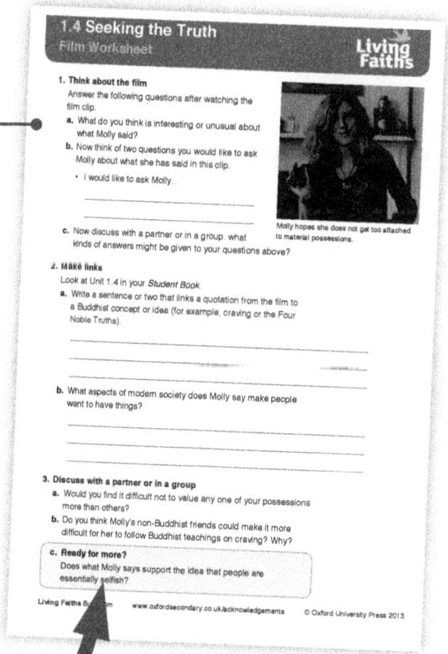

1.4 Seeking the Truth
Film Worksheet

1. Think about the film

Answer the following questions after watching the film clip.

a. What do you think is interesting or unusual about what Molly said?

b. Now think of two questions you would like to ask Molly about what she has said in this clip.

- I would like to ask Molly...

c. Now discuss with a partner or in a group: what kinds of answers might be given to your questions above?

Molly hopes she does not get too attached to material possessions.

2. Make links

Look at Unit 1.4 in your *Student Book*.

a. Write a sentence or two that links a quotation from the film to a Buddhist concept or idea (for example, craving or the Four Noble Truths).

b. What aspects of modern society does Molly say make people want to have things?

3. Discuss with a partner or in a group

a. Would you find it difficult not to value any one of your possessions more than others?

b. Do you think Molly's non-Buddhist friends could make it more difficult for her to follow Buddhist teachings on craving? Why?

c. **Ready for more?**
Does what Molly says support the idea that people are essentially selfish?

Living Faiths B... www.oxfordsecondary.co.uk/acknowledgements © Oxford University Press 2013

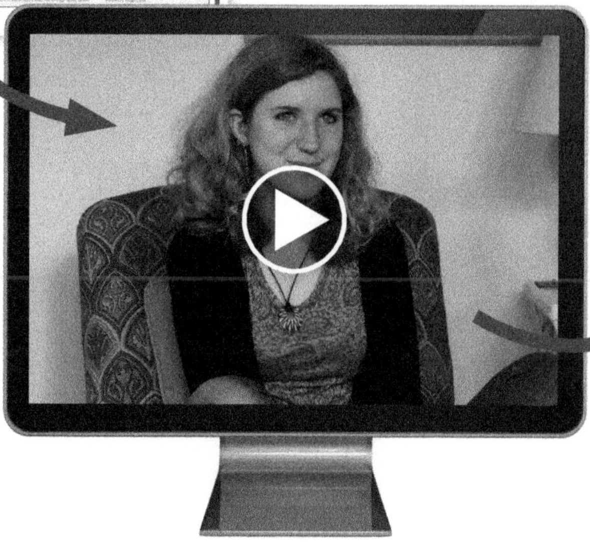

All the resources and assessments are **fully integrated** with the *Buddhism Student Book*

Kerboodle

Lesson presentations

Click on the **Lessons tab** to access the full list of *Living Faiths Buddhism* lessons and notes.

🎓 **Ready-to-play lesson presentations** complement every unit in the book. Each lesson presentation is easy to launch, and features unit objectives, the related starters, worksheets, film and interactive resources, and closes with a plenary activity or reflection. You can further **personalize** the lessons by adding in your own resources and notes. Your lessons and notes can be accessed by your whole department, and they are a great time-saver and **ideal for non-specialist** teachers and cover lessons.

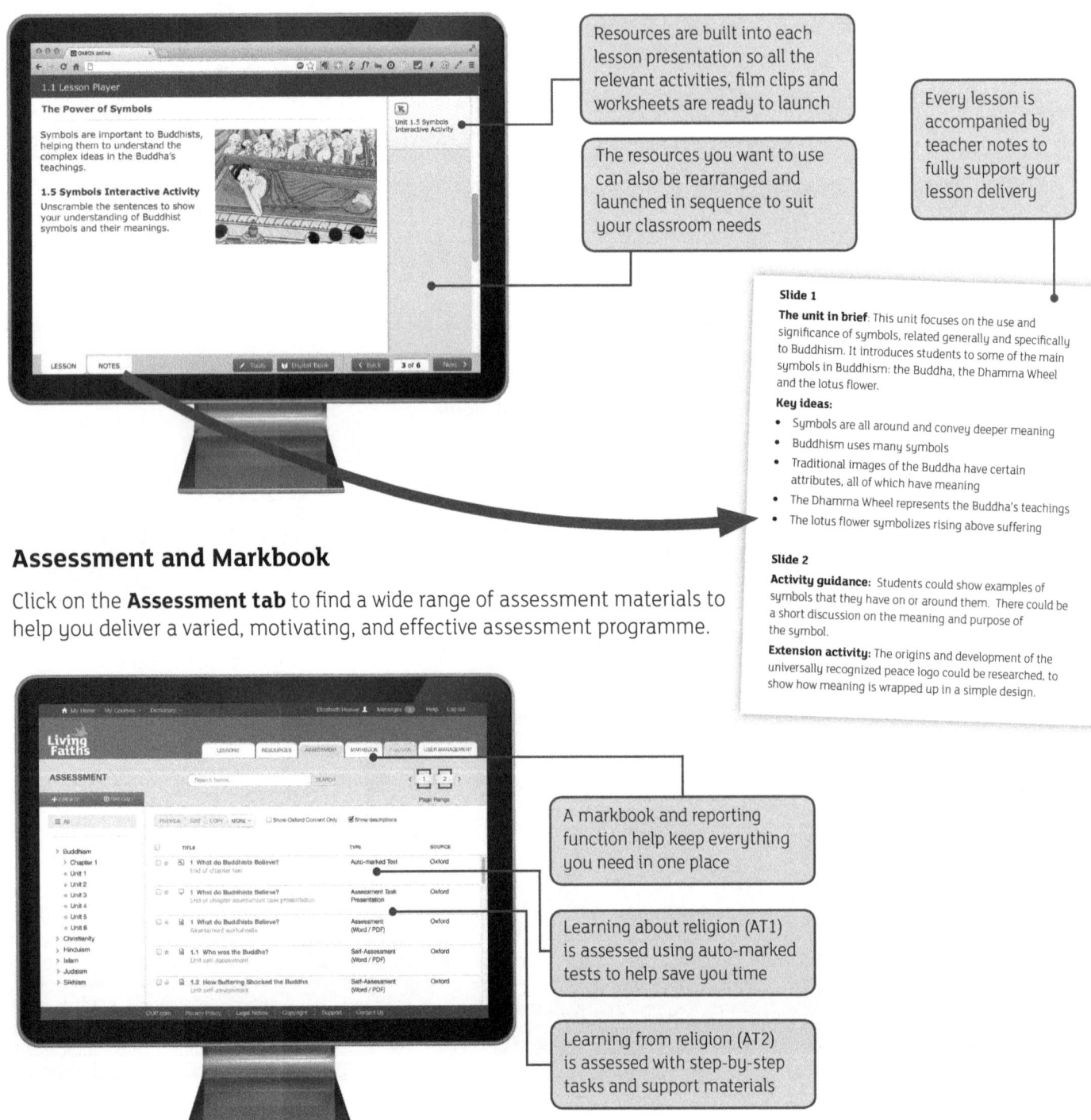

Resources are built into each lesson presentation so all the relevant activities, film clips and worksheets are ready to launch

The resources you want to use can also be rearranged and launched in sequence to suit your classroom needs

Every lesson is accompanied by teacher notes to fully support your lesson delivery

Slide 1

The unit in brief: This unit focuses on the use and significance of symbols, related generally and specifically to Buddhism. It introduces students to some of the main symbols in Buddhism: the Buddha, the Dhamma Wheel and the lotus flower.

Key ideas:

- Symbols are all around and convey deeper meaning
- Buddhism uses many symbols
- Traditional images of the Buddha have certain attributes, all of which have meaning
- The Dhamma Wheel represents the Buddha's teachings
- The lotus flower symbolizes rising above suffering

Slide 2

Activity guidance: Students could show examples of symbols that they have on or around them. There could be a short discussion on the meaning and purpose of the symbol.

Extension activity: The origins and development of the universally recognized peace logo could be researched, to show how meaning is wrapped up in a simple design.

Assessment and Markbook

Click on the **Assessment tab** to find a wide range of assessment materials to help you deliver a varied, motivating, and effective assessment programme.

A markbook and reporting function help keep everything you need in one place

Learning about religion (AT1) is assessed using auto-marked tests to help save you time

Learning from religion (AT2) is assessed with step-by-step tasks and support materials

The Assessment section provides:

- **2 baseline tests:** These tests cover both **Attainment Target 1** (learning *about* religion) and **Attainment Target 2** (learning *from* religion), and they can help you to quickly assess the prior RE knowledge that your new KS3 students may have.

- **5 auto-marked tests:** Each end-of-chapter auto-marked test assesses **AT1**. The marks are automatically reported in the **Markbook tab**.

- **30 self-assessment worksheets:** Self-assessment worksheets help students to self- or peer-evaluate the skills they have learnt from each unit.

- **5 assessment task presentations:** Each end-of-chapter assessment task in the *Student Book*, which assesses **AT2**, has a front-of-class presentation for you to use to help guide students towards understanding and analysing what the question/task is asking of them. You can lead students through this step-by-step presentation and help them decide how to prepare to answer the question.

- **15 assessment worksheets:** These worksheets complement the assessment tasks in the *Student Book* and the assessment task presentations. They recap the task, provide a self-evaluation chart, and space for students to prepare their work.

A **Markbook** with reporting function completes the *Kerboodle* assessment package, so you can keep track of all your students' test results and assessment scores. This includes both the auto-marked tests and work that need to be marked by you. It is also easy to import class registers and create user accounts for all your students.

Kerboodle Book

The **Buddhism Kerboodle Book** provides you with an on-screen version of the *Student Book* for you to use on your whiteboard with the whole class.

Teacher access to the *Kerboodle Book* is **automatically available** as part of the Lessons, Resources and Assessment package. You can also choose to buy access for your students.

Both teacher and student access include a simple bank of tools so you can personalize the book and take notes.

It can be accessed on other devices, such as tablets.

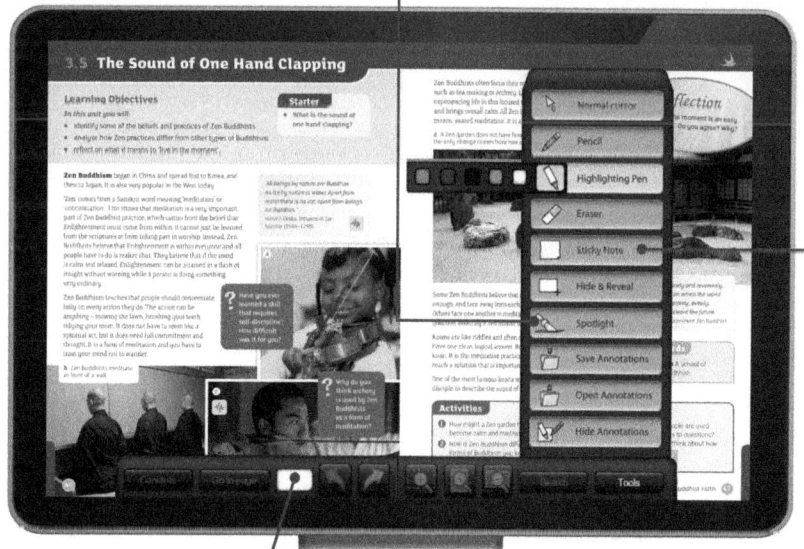

Zoom in and spotlight any part of the text

Use different tools such as Sticky Notes, Bookmarks and Pencil features to personalize each page

Navigate around the book quickly with the contents menu, keyword search or page number search

Every teacher and student has their own digital notebook for use within their *Kerboodle Book*. You can even choose to share some of your notes with your students, or hide them from view – all student notes are accessible to themselves only

Chapter 1 Overview
What do Buddhists Believe?

Helping you deliver Key Stage 3 RE

This chapter addresses the following areas of the Programme of Study:

Key concepts

Beliefs, teachings and sources
- Understand and respond critically to beliefs and attitudes

Key processes

Learning about religion
- Apply a wide range of religious and philosophical vocabulary consistently and accurately
- Explain religious beliefs and practices, including their transmission by people and traditions

Learning from religion
- Reflect on the relationship between beliefs, teachings and ultimate questions

The big picture

These are the key ideas behind this chapter:

- Prince Siddattha Gotama renounced his privileged life and later became known as the Buddha.
- In the real world Siddattha was deeply shocked by old age, sickness, death and a holy life. He decided to try to find a way to end suffering.
- The Buddha found Enlightenment through meditation and taught about the Three Signs of Being: anicca, dukkha and anatta.
- The Four Noble Truths explain that suffering is inevitable, but if people take the Middle Way and stop craving things, suffering will end.
- Buddhism uses specific symbols to represent ideas and convey deeper meaning.
- Buddhists believe that the choices they make in life build up positive or negative kamma (karma), which affects how they are reborn.

Chapter outline

Use this to give students a mental roadmap for the chapter:

1.1 Who was the Buddha? – introduces Siddattha Gotama and his early life

1.2 How Suffering Shocked the Buddha – explains how the sights Siddattha saw changed his life and prompted him to try to find a way to end suffering in the world

1.3 Everything Changes: The Three Signs of Being – explains how the Buddha found Enlightenment and introduces the Three Signs of Being; includes a case study

1.4 Seeking the Truth – explores the Four Noble Truths, how suffering is caused by craving and how craving can be 'cured' by taking the Middle Way; includes a case study

1.5 Symbols: Making Meaning – explores the use and meaning of some key symbols in Buddhism

1.6 Good or Bad – It's Your Choice – introduces Buddhist beliefs on life, death and rebirth, and explores the meaning and importance of kamma through case studies

Opportunities for assessment

Baseline auto-marked test and assessment tasks are available on the *Buddhism Kerboodle*. These allow you to evaluate how much knowledge students already have about Buddhism before you start the course.

Summative assessments on the *Buddhism Kerboodle* include auto-marked tests, interactive activities and self-assessment worksheets.

The end-of-chapter assessment task in the *Student Book* provides formative assessment. Supporting materials for the assessment task can be found on the *Buddhism Kerboodle*, such as the Assessment Task Presentation and related worksheets.

There are other opportunities for assessment too. For example, you could use some of the activities or reflection points throughout each *Student Book* unit, or some of the 'Further suggestions' at the end of this chapter.

Getting ready for this chapter

Familiarize yourself with the teachings of the Buddha on suffering, the Three Signs of Being, the Four Noble Truths, and kamma, so that you can encourage in-depth discussion.

If you have the *Buddhism Kerboodle*, watch the case study film clips in advance so that you can prepare and guide students before and during their viewing.

If possible, you could arrange a visit to a local Buddhist centre or temple at some point during the course.

You might find it useful to obtain a collection of Buddhist artefacts and images to use as learning aids, such as small statues or images of the Buddha in different positions and various interpretations of the Dhamma Wheel (Dhammacakka).

You could start this course by asking students to consolidate prior learning by creating a spider diagram or mind-map of what they already know about Buddhism.

If possible, check out IMDb's (Internet Movie Database's) website, and search for *The Matrix*. 'Watch Trailer' runs a visual overview of the film, explaining the key concepts. You could show this trailer when the class discusses living in the real world as opposed to living a sheltered life. The film is rated '15' so you might need to seek parental permission to screen the entire film.

Objectives and outcomes for this chapter

Objectives	Unit	Outcomes
Most students will:		Most students will be able to:
• investigate who the Buddha was • respond to the story of his early life • reflect on aspects of their own lives.	1.1	• explain who the Buddha was • evaluate the Buddha's decision to try to find out about the real world • express an opinion on how much lives in Britain are sheltered.
• understand the impact of the Four Sights on Siddattha • reflect on how human beings are affected by suffering • reflect on the different types of suffering around them.	1.2	• describe the impact of the Four Sights on Siddattha • identify other possible responses to suffering in the world • identify different types of physical and mental suffering in the world.
• explore the meaning of anicca, dukkha and anatta • explain how the Three Signs of Being led to the Buddha's Enlightenment • reflect on the Buddha's teachings about change, suffering and the self.	1.3	• explain the meaning of anicca, dukkha and anatta, and identify examples of dukkha • put the Three Signs of Being into context in the world as they know it • say whether they think the Buddha's teachings on change, suffering and self might help them.
• explore the Four Noble Truths • analyse the causes and effects of craving things • reflect on their own views about wanting things.	1.4	• identify and describe the Four Noble Truths • identify the causes and effects of craving things, and explain the links between craving and suffering • express their views about wanting things and if they would have a better life with less.
• identify what symbols mean and why they are important • explain some important symbols for Buddhists • reflect on the significance of symbols in everyday life.	1.5	• explain what symbols mean and why they are important • explain the meaning of important Buddhist symbols and design their own • explain the significance of symbols in their own lives and say how one Buddhist symbol makes them feel.
• examine Buddhist beliefs about life, death and rebirth • explain the meaning and importance of kamma • reflect on the effects of their actions on themselves and others.	1.6	• explain Buddhist beliefs about life, death and rebirth • explain Buddhist beliefs about kamma and say how such a belief might affect their own lives • say how they want to be remembered.

1.1 Who was the Buddha?

The unit in brief

This unit introduces the Buddha and his life as Prince Siddattha Gotama. It considers the importance of being a spiritual leader and the value of living a sheltered life.

Key ideas

- The Buddha was born an Indian prince, 2500 years ago
- A Buddha is a person who discovers Enlightenment for themself rather than from the teachings of others
- The Buddha led a sheltered life in a palace but wanted to know about the real world outside
- Being a spiritual leader might be just as important as being a leader in the material world
- Many people in Britain live sheltered lives

Skills practised

- Literacy: reading independently
- Evaluation: considering whether being a spiritual leader is as important as being a leader in the material world
- Reflection: considering whether it's better to live a sheltered life or one that involves all the problems of the real world
- Speaking: delivering a speech and contributing to a debate

Resources

- 📄 1.1 Comic Strip Worksheet: students design a comic strip depicting the early life of Prince Siddattha
- 🔝 1.1 Siddattha Interactive Activity: students complete sentences describing the story of Siddattha's early life
- 🎓 1.1 Lesson Player: a ready-to-go presentation with built-in resources and teacher notes
- 🖥 1 Image Gallery: a useful gallery of photos and illustrations from the chapter
- 📄 1.1 Self-Assessment Sheet: students evaluate their learning against the lesson objectives

Ideas for starters

1. Display the picture of the Buddha in the *Student Book* as students enter the room. Use the starters in the *Student Book*, sharing responses.
2. Ask students whether their parents or friends have ever hidden something from them, for example, in order to keep them safe.

Explain that they are going to be learning about someone who was completely hidden away from the 'real world'.

3. Ask students if they know any details about the early life of one of their heroes or of any famous political or spiritual leaders. Share feedback. Ask why they think it is useful to know about someone's early life.

Activity guidance

- For Activity **1** in the *Student Book*, make sure students understand the use of the word 'spiritual'. Emphasize that it does not refer to ghosts or the afterlife.

- A traditional example of a story for Activity **3** in the *Student Book* would be *Sleeping Beauty*, in which the king sends his daughter away to try to protect her. In *The Matrix*, Neo learns that the 'reality' experienced by most of the characters is in fact simulated, and rebels against the machines that created it. Similarly, in *The Truman show*, Truman feels that life is too perfect and suspects that something is being hidden from him (which it is).

Ideas for plenaries

1. Use the Reflection from the *Student Book*.

2. If students have written a speech for Activity **2**, ask one or more to deliver their speeches at the end of the lesson.

3. Organize a class debate on the question in Activity **2**. Elect a chairperson. At the end, take a vote. Ask students to write one sentence to justify their decision.

4. Ask students to explain to a partner, in one sentence, why the life of the Buddha is important to Buddhists.

Further class and homework activities

1. You could use 1.1 Comic Strip Worksheet on the *Buddhism Kerboodle* at the end of the lesson as a creative way to consolidate knowledge. By creating a cartoon strip, students will show that they have an understanding of the early life of Siddattha Gotama and that they can analyse the important events of his early life.

2. 1.1 Siddattha Interactive Activity on the *Buddhism Kerboodle*.

3. Further suggestions on page 28 of this book.

1.2 How Suffering Shocked the Buddha

The unit in brief

This unit explains what happened on Siddattha's journey outside the palace. It introduces the Four Sights and encourages students to empathize with their impact on Siddattha. It prompts students to reflect on the effects of suffering in the world.

Key ideas

- Siddattha saw Four Sights that had a huge impact on him: an old man, a sick man, a funeral, and a holy man
- He decided to lead a spiritual life to find a way to end the suffering in the world
- Suffering of one type or another is all around us in this world

Useful Words

Four Sights, samana

Skills practised

- Literacy: reading independently
- Empathy: understanding the impact of the Four Sights on Siddattha
- Thinking: considering what things shock us and the different types of suffering
- Reflection: considering how people are affected by suffering

Resources

- ⌁ 1.2 Story Audio Clip: a reading of the story of the Four Sights that features in the *Student Book*

- 📄 1.2 Letter Worksheet: students write a letter as if they were Siddattha, explaining their decision to leave or stay in the palace

- 🔲 1.2 Four Sights Interactive Activity: students identify the Four Sights that led to Siddattha's decision to become a samana

- 🎓 1.2 Lesson Player: a ready-to-go presentation with built-in resources and teacher notes

- 🖼 1 Image Gallery: a useful gallery of photos and illustrations from the chapter

- 📄 1.2 Self-Assessment Sheet: students evaluate their learning against the lesson objectives

Ideas for starters

1. Ask students to write one thing that shocks them on a sticky note and stick it on the board. Share some of the ideas and develop a brief discussion on why and how some things shock and others do not.

2. Ask students to write ideas as above, but put all the notes in a box. Ask them to take notes out randomly and then form a continuum line, ordering how shocking they find the events on the sticky notes. Ask students to share their reasoning.

Activity guidance

- For Activity **2** in the *Student Book*, make sure students understand that they should use the different types of suffering mentioned in Samyutta Nikaya 56:11 to inform their mind-map.

Ideas for plenaries

1. Use the Reflection from the *Student Book*.

2. Ask students to write three sentences to explain what they have learned from this unit.

3. Ask students to prepare a short piece of writing starting with 'I do/do not think we can solve the problem of suffering in the world because…'.

4. Ask students to explain to a partner, in one minute, whether they think the Buddha was right about all life being suffering.

Further class and homework activities

1. Ask students to imagine that they are interviewing Siddattha after he saw the Four Sights. What five questions would they like to ask him about what he saw?

2. Ask students to write a shock newspaper report under the headline: 'Shock as Buddha reveals all life is suffering!'

3. You could use 1.2 Letter Worksheet on the *Buddhism Kerboodle* at the end of the lesson or as a homework. When they are finished they could 'send' their letter to a classmate.

4. 1.2 Four Sights Interactive Activity on the *Buddhism Kerboodle*.

5. Further suggestions on page 28 of this book.

1.3 Everything Changes: The Three Signs of Being

The unit in brief

This unit tells the story of how the Buddha found Enlightenment. It introduces the Three Signs of Being: anicca, dukkha and anatta. It also encourages students to think about what makes them who they are as people.

Key ideas

- The Buddha found Enlightenment through meditation and began to teach people how they could free themselves from suffering
- Anicca means that everything changes and nothing lasts forever
- Dukkha is all types of physical and mental pain and suffering
- Anatta is the belief that there is no permanent self or soul

> **Useful Words**
>
> anatta, anicca, Bodhi tree, dhamma, dukkha, Enlightenment, Three Signs of Being

Skills practised

- Literacy: using key terms from another language with confidence
- Evaluation: considering the Buddha's teachings about change, suffering and the self
- Speaking: talking about what defines them as a person
- Reflection: considering what defines a person

Resources

- 1.3 Three Signs Film Clip A: Mrs Aldam considers the concept of anicca
- 1.3 Three Signs Film Clip B: Mrs Harvey talks about the nature of dukkha in life
- 1.3 Film Worksheet: students assess their understanding of the case study film clips by linking ideas to the *Student Book*
- 1.3 Terms Interactive Activity: students must match up the terms introduced in this unit to the correct definitions
- 1.3 Lesson Player: a ready-to-go presentation with built-in resources and teacher notes
- 1 Image Gallery: a useful gallery of photos and illustrations from the chapter
- 1.3 Self-Assessment Sheet: students evaluate their learning against the lesson objectives

Ideas for starters

1. Extend the first starter in the *Student Book* by asking students to create a mind-map on the questions. Encourage them to think of at least three or four ideas around the central word 'Me'.

2. Give students a few minutes to think about the first starter in the *Student Book*. Then organize a hot-seating activity, where those in the hot-seat speak for 30 seconds on their thoughts about the two questions.

3. Write 'Nothing lasts forever' on the board and instigate a class discussion on the idea.

4. On the board, list the meaning and connotations of the word 'Enlightenment'. Explain that students will hear a very specific meaning of it in the lesson and they should make a note of it.

Activity guidance

- Take the opportunity in Activity **1** in the *Student Book* to explore the concept of dukkha as extensively as possible. Encourage students to think creatively and beyond the obvious answers around physical suffering.

Ideas for plenaries

1. Use the Reflection from the *Student Book*.

2. Ask students to recap on the meaning of 'Enlightenment' in the context of Buddhism.

3. Ask students to learn the meaning of dhamma, anatta, dukkha and anicca for a quick test next lesson.

4. Remind students of the first starter in the *Student Book*. Ask them what they think about the Buddha's teachings about anicca and anatta, and how they impact on how they think of themselves as a person.

5. Ask students to present and explain their drawings for Activity **3** in the *Student Book*.

Further class and homework activities

1. Show students a range of examples of how different artists have interpreted the Buddha finding Enlightenment under the Bodhi tree and discuss the differences. Ask students to draw their own picture of this event. They should identify what qualities they want to convey about this experience.

2. 1.3 Film Worksheet on the *Buddhism Kerboodle*.

3. 1.3 Terms Interactive Activity on the *Buddhism Kerboodle*.

4. Further suggestions on page 28 of this book.

1.4 Seeking the Truth

The unit in brief

This unit introduces students to the Buddha's Four Noble Truths. It explains that dukkha is caused by selfish craving and that this can cease by taking the 'Middle Way'. A practising Buddhist also gives their personal experience of trying to avoid craving.

Key ideas

- The Buddha taught the Four Noble Truths
- All life involves suffering/dukkha, and selfish craving causes dukkha
- If people stop craving things, dukkha will end: the 'cure' is to take the Middle Way by following the Noble Eightfold Path
- Giving up craving is very difficult

Useful Words

craving, Four Noble Truths, Middle Way

Skills practised

- Interpretation: explaining the significance of the Four Noble Truths
- Analysis: considering the causes and effects of craving and why it is so difficult to let go of things
- Reflection: considering their own views about wanting things
- Literacy: writing a short speech about craving things
- Communication: drawing a storyboard

Resources

- 1.4 Craving Film Clip: Molly discusses the problems of trying to avoid craving things in modern-day Britain
- 1.4 Film Worksheet: students assess their understanding of the case study film clips by linking ideas to the *Student Book*
- 1.4 Noble Truths Interactive Activity: students fill the gaps in a paragraph about the Four Noble Truths
- 1.4 Lesson Player: a ready-to-go presentation with built-in resources and teacher notes
- 1 Image Gallery: a useful gallery of photos and illustrations from the chapter
- 1.4 Self-Assessment Sheet: students evaluate their learning against the lesson objectives

Ideas for starters

1. Use one or both of the starters from the *Student Book* to spark discussion.

2. Ask students what they understand by the word 'truth'. Draw out that as well as being a provable fact or reality, as opposed to a falsehood, it can have a broader meaning: a belief about how something is or how something should be, which comes from experience, but is not exactly provable.

3. Ask students for truthful statements. They must explain how they know their suggestion is truthful.

Activity guidance

- After students have completed Activity **2** in the *Student Book*, ask them to read and improve their speeches with the help of a partner. Then, either ask individuals to give their speeches to the class, or develop the topic into a class debate.

- Use Activity **3** in the *Student Book* to take the opportunity to explore, as a class, the concepts of the Four Noble Truths and the links between selfishness, craving and suffering.

- For Activity **4** in the *Student Book* encourage students to base their stories on something that they can identify with, such as wanting the latest bicycle, mobile phone or tablet computer. How would they feel if they were told they could not have the thing they wanted most? Why?

Ideas for plenaries

1. Use the Reflection from the *Student Book*.

2. Ask students to learn the Four Noble Truths for a quick test next lesson.

3. Give students a few minutes to work in pairs and compile three questions they want to ask the Buddha about the Four Noble Truths. Share the questions and agree on a shortlist of the best three to five questions.

4. Ask students to show and explain their storyboards for Activity **4** in the *Student Book* in small groups.

Further class and homework activities

1. 1.4 Film Worksheet on the *Buddhism Kerboodle*.

2. 1.4 Noble Truths Interactive Activity on the *Buddhism Kerboodle*.

3. Further suggestions on page 28 of this book.

1.5 Symbols: Making Meaning

The unit in brief

This unit focuses on the use and significance of symbols, related generally and specifically to Buddhism. It introduces students to some of the main symbols in Buddhism: the Buddha, the Dhamma Wheel and the lotus flower.

Key ideas

- Symbols are all around and convey deeper meaning
- Buddhism uses many symbols
- Traditional images of the Buddha have certain attributes, all of which have meaning
- The Dhamma Wheel represents the Buddha's teachings
- The lotus flower symbolizes rising above suffering

Useful Words

Dhamma Wheel (Dhammacakka), lotus flower

Skills practised

- Enquiry: identifying symbols, their meanings and importance
- Interpretation: explaining Buddhist symbols
- Evaluation: considering symbols that best represent Buddhism
- Communication: drawing a symbol to communicate key teachings
- Reflection: considering the impact of a Buddhist symbol on their feelings

Resources

- 〰 1.5 Music Audio Clip: Some traditional Japanese flute music to be used with Activity **3** in the *Student Book*

- 📄 1.5 Symbols Worksheet: students identify and discuss the effectiveness of Buddhist symbols

- 🖱 1.5 Symbolism Interactive Activity: students link descriptions of the Buddha or Buddhist symbols to their correct meanings

- 🏠 1.5 Lesson Player: a ready-to-go presentation with built-in resources and teacher notes

- 🖥 1 Image Gallery: a useful gallery of photos and illustrations from the chapter

- 📄 1.5 Self-Assessment Sheet: students evaluate their learning against the lesson objectives

Ideas for starters

1. Display the picture of the peace symbol in the *Student Book* as students enter the room. Ask: what does this logo say to you? Then explain the features and value of logos.

2. Use the starters in the *Student Book*, sharing responses.

3. Ask students to look through their bags or pencil cases to see how many symbols or logos they can find. Share answers to the question.

4. Ask students which symbols they like the most and why. Try to identify specific features. Lead into the second starter in the *Student Book*. Consider design, colour and effectiveness of the message.

5. Ask students to sketch one symbol they think is very effective. Choose students to present their choice and reasons to the class.

Activity guidance

*   For Activity **1** in the *Student Book*, pairs could join to make groups of four to explain their reasoning and agree on the best symbol. Alternatively, you could ask a few students to explain their views and then take a class vote.

*   The symbols students designed for Activity **2** in the *Student Book* could form the basis of a wall display.

*   For Activity **3** in the *Student Book* you will need to insist on quiet or you could play some Buddhist music softly in the background to provide a contemplative atmosphere. Share and compare their reactions. For homework, you could ask students to write a short thoughtful description or poem about how they felt about the symbol.

*   Try to arrange for the head teacher or a senior member of staff to do a ten-minute hot-seat session for Activity **4** in the *Student Book*. Ask students to write up their notes on the responses for homework. They could also draw the school badge or logo and label it to explain its meaning.

*   For more about symbols in another faith see Unit 2.1 in the *Hinduism Student Book*.

Ideas for plenaries

1. Use the Reflection from the *Student Book*.

2. Nominate students to explain their designs for Activity **2** in the *Student Book* to the class. Remind them to refer to Buddhist teaching.

3. Take and discuss feedback from Activity **3** in the *Student Book*.

Further class and homework activities

1. You could use 1.5 Symbols Worksheet on the *Buddhism Kerboodle* at the end of the lesson to consolidate knowledge and encourage higher ability students to do some further research.

2. 1.5 Symbolism Interactive Activity on the *Buddhism Kerboodle*.

3. Further suggestions on page 28 of this book.

1.6 Good or Bad – It's Your Choice

The unit in brief

This unit introduces Buddhist beliefs on life, death and rebirth. It explains the meaning and importance of kamma (karma). Students have the opportunity to reflect on their own views on death and the effects of their actions on themselves and others.

Key ideas

- Death is inevitable so it is important to make life special
- Buddhists believe that how they live affects what happens after death
- Buddhists believe that after death all living things are reborn according to kamma
- Kamma refers to the actions resulting from the choices people make and can be positive or negative
- The endless cycle of birth and rebirth is called samsara
- The only escape from samsara is to follow the Buddha's teachings and seek Enlightenment

Useful Words

impermanence, kamma, samsara

Skills practised

- Thinking: considering the things they want to be remembered for
- Enquiry: examining Buddhist beliefs on life, death, rebirth and kamma
- Literacy: using key terms in another language with confidence, and writing an email
- Reflection: considering the effects of their actions on themselves and others
- Interpretation: explaining the meaning and importance of kamma

Resources

- 1.6 Kamma Film Clip A: Mrs Aldam considers how kamma helps her make sense of life
- 1.6 Kamma Film Clip B: Mrs Harvey explains her belief that all actions have consequences
- 1.6 Film Worksheet: students assess their understanding of the case study film clips by linking ideas to the *Student Book*
- 1.6 Cycle of Life Interactive Activity: students select statements about life, death and rebirth that reflect Buddhist beliefs
- 1.6 Lesson Player: a ready-to-go presentation with built-in resources and teacher notes
- 1 Image Gallery: a useful gallery of photos and illustrations from the chapter
- 1.6 Self-Assessment Sheet: students evaluate their learning against the lesson objectives

Ideas for starters

1. Use the first starter in the *Student Book*, extending it by asking students to list words that they would like to be used to describe the way they have lived.

2. Use the second starter in the *Student Book*.

3. Ask students to list all the things they would like to do before they die.

4. Give students one minute to discuss in pairs what they understand by the term 'rebirth'. Then encourage students to share their ideas with the class.

5. Discuss what students believe about life after death.

Activity guidance

- For Activity **1** in the *Student Book*, prompt students to think of any good things that they have done, such as acts of kindness to siblings and friends or occasions when they have had to work hard for something. Draw out that even relatively small actions like this have positive consequences. Move on to discuss the difficulties and consequences of making more difficult decisions such as refusing to copy a friend's wrong-doings.

- To compare Buddhist teaching with Hindu beliefs about karma, see Unit 3.1 in the *Hinduism Student Book*.

Ideas for plenaries

1. Use the Reflection from the *Student Book*.

2. Ask students to learn the meaning of kamma and samsara for a quick test next lesson.

3. 'Belief in kamma affects the way Buddhists live.' Ask students to write a response to this statement in no more than 50 words.

4. Choose a student to hot-seat and answer the questions prepared in Activity **4** in the *Student Book* as if they are Mrs Aldam or Mrs Harvey.

Further class and homework activities

1. Ask students to think about what influences them in decisions about actions they take. Are they influenced by parents or friends, for example? Encourage them to consider the influence of wider culture and the media. Then evaluate the Buddhist belief that actions determine whether you build up good or bad kamma.

2. You could use 1.6 Film Worksheet on the *Buddhism Kerboodle* after watching the film clips in order to extend students' understanding of kamma.

3. 1.6 Cycle of Life Interactive Activity on the *Buddhism Kerboodle*.

4. Further suggestions on page 28 of this book.

Chapter 1 Further Suggestions

These suggestions are addressed directly to students.

1.1 Who was the Buddha?

1 Research more about the life of the Buddha. Make a poster or leaflet based on your findings. **

2 Create a film trailer storyboard about the early life of Siddattha Gotama. If you can, you could even film your trailer. *

3 Write your own story about somebody who grows up living a privileged life. Think about what they would be like and how they would feel about their life. **

4 Do some research into stories about the early lives of other key religious figures, for example, Jesus, Moses, Guru Nanak, or Lord Krishna. Identify some characteristics of these stories. Why is it important for religions to have stories like these about their leaders? ***

1.2 How Suffering Shocked the Buddha

1 Find out more about the samanas and how they lived. **

2 Research how different groups and individuals respond to suffering in the world. ***

3 Find out about a Buddhist charity that helps those in need. **

1.3 Everything Changes: The Three Signs of Being

1 Look through old newspapers and cut out words and stories to make a collage of examples of dukkha. *

2 'For things to be truly beautiful, they have to one day cease to exist.' Write a response to this statement. **

3 Do you agree with the Buddha when he says that we have no 'soul'? Write a speech arguing for or against the existence of the soul. ***

1.4 Seeking the Truth

1 List all the things that would be difficult for you to let go of. Give each a number according to how attached you feel you are to each thing, with number 1 being the thing you would find most difficult to let go. *

2 Create a flow chart to show the Four Noble Truths. Add pictures and labels to show the relationship between craving and dukkha. ***

3 Do you think that following the Middle Way is good for people regardless of whether or not they are Buddhist? Write a short explanation of your views, giving examples. **

1.5 Symbols: Making Meaning

1 Research symbols from some other faiths you have studied. Make a poster, showing the symbols from each faith and explaining what they mean. **

2 'Pictures are more powerful than words.' In small groups, debate this statement. **

3 Find more pictures of the Dhammacakka. Are there any differences? What do you think they might represent? Can you think of any reasons for the differences? ***

4 Create a leaflet for visitors to a Buddhist temple that explains the meaning of the images and symbols they will see. **

1.6 Good or Bad – It's Your Choice

1 In small groups, discuss times when you have seen, heard or read about kamma in action. **

2 'All actions have consequences.' Discuss whether this statement is always true or not. **

3 Choose one other faith and make notes about its beliefs about death. Then write an extended paragraph that explores a key similarity to, or difference from, Buddhism. Explain why you think this is significant. ***

Chapter 1 Assessment

Assessment in the *Student Book*

You will find an assessment task at the end of every chapter that focuses on AT2. In this chapter, the task asks students to design a poster that explains the Four Noble Truths, using images and quotations.

In the *Student Book* (and on the supporting worksheets), you'll find guidance about levels of assessment that you can use to help your students understand what their work should include. You could ask them to use these criteria for self- or peer-assessment once they've completed the task.

Living Faiths Assessment
Student Book
• Assessment Task
• Levels Guidance
Kerboodle
• Auto-Marked Test
• Assessment Task Presentation
• Assessment Worksheets

Assessment Task for Chapter 1 (pages **20–21** of the *Buddhism Student Book*)

Objectives

- Examine the Four Noble Truths and the effect they have on Buddhists' lives.
- Interpret the teachings of the Buddha for modern life.
- Reflect on your own ideas about whether there is a cure for the suffering in the world.

Task

Design and make a poster for a doctor's surgery waiting room. On the poster, explain the symptoms of the 'illness' the Buddha said people are suffering from, and what the cure is. Include specific religious terms, but also be clear and straightforward so that it can be understood by everyone. You could include some Buddhist symbols or images to show that the poster is based on Buddhist teachings. You could also include some quotations from this chapter. Make a note of your thoughts so you can share them in a class discussion.

Assessment in *Kerboodle*

On the *Buddhism Kerboodle*, you'll find resources to use when introducing the assessment task to the class.

You can use the *Chapter 1 Assessment Task Presentation* as a front-of-class tool to help your students unpack the assessment criteria, and understand what is expected of them.

Chapter 1 Assessment Worksheets accompany the task, so that once you finish the presentation, your students can easily get started.

Auto-marked tests

The *Buddhism Kerboodle* also contains auto-marked tests for each chapter to help save you time setting questions and marking for AT1. The test for this chapter contains 15 questions and will take most students about half an hour. Test results are automatically stored in the markbook.

Digital markbook

A markbook and a reporting function complete the *Kerboodle* assessment package, so you can keep all your students' test results and assessment scores in one place. This can include the auto-marked tests as well as pieces of work you or the students have marked by hand.

▲ Assessment resources for Chapter 1 on the *Buddhism Kerboodle*

Chapter 2 Overview
Where do Buddhist Beliefs Come From?

Helping you deliver Key Stage 3 RE

This chapter addresses the following areas of the Programme of Study:

Key concepts

Beliefs, teachings and sources
- Interpret teachings, sources, authorities and ways of life in order to understand religions and beliefs

Practices and ways of life
- Explore the impact of religions and beliefs on how people live their lives

Meaning purpose and truth
- Explore some of the ultimate questions that confront humanity, and respond imaginatively to them

Key processes

Learning about religion
- Explain religious beliefs, practices and commitments, including their transmission by people, texts and traditions

Learning from religion
- Reflect on the relationship between beliefs, teachings and ultimate questions

The big picture

These are the key ideas behind this chapter:

- Scripture provides a clear framework for Buddhists to live by but how Buddhists choose to live is also very important.
- Stories can be very effective in conveying a deeper meaning or moral.
- The Buddha taught that Enlightenment can be found by following the Middle Way and that it leads to Nibbana (Nirvana), the state of perfect peace.
- Buddhists try to live by the Five Precepts and other guidelines, and believe that positive actions create positive kamma.
- Celebrations help believers to feel part of the religious community.
- Buddhists believe in rebirth, which is influenced by kamma.
- Buddhists pay respect to the Buddha, and that worship takes many forms.

Chapter outline

Use this to give students a mental roadmap for the chapter:

2.1 Read All About It! – explores the idea of authority and how important scripture is to Buddhists

2.2 How can Stories Inspire? – looks at one moral tale from the Buddhist tradition and explores its meaning and the value of moral stories

2.3 Which is the Right Path? – introduces the Noble Eightfold Path, which is the Buddhist guide for living, and explores its practical application through a case study

2.4 The Five Precepts – focuses on Buddhist moral codes and includes a case study

2.5 Let's Celebrate! – focuses on Wesak, and how and why it is celebrated, using a case study

2.6 Life and Death: The Never-Ending Circle – explores Buddhist beliefs around life, death and rebirth

2.7 Can You Worship Without a God? – explores the meaning of worship to Buddhists, including through case studies

Opportunities for assessment

Summative assessments on the *Buddhism Kerboodle* include auto-marked tests, interactive activities and self-assessment worksheets.

The end-of-chapter assessment task in the *Student Book* provides formative assessment. Supporting materials for the assessment task can be found on the *Buddhism Kerboodle*, such as the Assessment Task Presentation and related worksheets.

There are other opportunities for assessment too. For example, you could use some of the activities or reflection points throughout each *Student Book* unit, or some of the 'Further suggestions' at the end of this chapter.

Getting ready for this chapter

Familiarize yourself with some of the Jataka Tales and the teachings of the Buddha on the Middle Way, the Noble Eightfold Path and samsara so that you can encourage in-depth discussion.

You might find it useful to make a collection of Buddhist artefacts and images to aid you in your teaching. If you wish to celebrate Wesak Day, as suggested in Unit 2.5, you could source a small statue of the Buddha, some tea lights and small bowls to carry scented water. Students will also need access to a selection of the Jataka Tales for Unit 2.2.

You might also consider setting up a shrine in preparation for Unit 2.7. Performing puja should be acceptable given that the intention is to educate. Buddhist parents or members of a local Buddhist community may be willing to share their own practice.

Objectives and outcomes for this chapter

Objectives	Unit	Outcomes
Most students will:		Most students will be able to:
• evaluate the importance of scripture to religious believers • explain how and why Buddhists use key scriptures • reflect on the nature of religious wisdom and life experience.	2.1	• explain why people find guidelines in life useful • explain how Buddhists follow the Middle Way and why this concept is central to Buddhism • evaluate the value of human wisdom, scripture and human experience.
• explain the importance of the Jataka Tales for Buddhists • reflect on the meaning behind a story.	2.2	• say how useful stories are in giving moral messages • evaluate the importance of the Jataka Tales for Buddhists • ask questions about the meaning of the story of the Monkey King.
• analyse the Buddha's teaching on finding the right way • find out about how Buddhists try to shape their lives according to the Buddha's teachings • reflect on the idea of a world without suffering.	2.3	• explain the Middle Way and the Noble Eightfold Path • relate the difficulties practising Buddhists have in trying to live according to the Buddha's teachings • debate what a world without suffering would be like.
• identify the features of the Five Precepts • identify ways of following Buddhist guidelines in everyday life • reflect on how easy it is to change actions and behaviour.	2.4	• explain the Five Precepts • suggest how difficult it might be to follow the Five Precepts and how they might overcome the challenges • consider personal guidelines for life and how easy it might be to change actions and behaviour.
• investigate a special day for Buddhists • identify the main features of the Buddhist festival of Wesak • reflect on their own ideas about religious celebrations.	2.5	• explain what happens at Wesak and why • compare secular and other religious celebrations, identifying similarities • explain their own ideas about whether non-believers should celebrate religious festivals.
• examine Buddhist beliefs on life and death • explore the concepts of samsara and Nibbana • reflect on the impermanence of life.	2.6	• explain Buddhist beliefs about life, death and rebirth • show understanding of the concepts of samsara and Nibbana through writing an obituary for the Buddha • make links with other faiths' views on death.
• identify what worship means • investigate different types of Buddhist worship • reflect on the idea of worship without a god.	2.7	• explain what worship means • write a clear guide on different types of Buddhist worship • justify their view on whether someone can be spiritual without being religious.

2.1 Read All About It!

The unit in brief

This unit explores what is meant by authority and introduces the different collections of Buddhist teachings. It looks at how important scripture is to Buddhists. Students are prompted to think about the sources of authority in their own lives and the nature of religious wisdom and life experience.

Key ideas

- Many religious believers find authority in scripture
- The Buddha's teachings were passed down by word of mouth and then collected into the Sanskrit and Pali Canons – the Pali Canon is known as the Tipitaka (Three Baskets)
- The Vinaya basket contains rules for ordained Buddhists, the Sutta basket contains the main teachings of the Buddha, and the Abhidhamma basket contains more philosophical teachings
- Scripture provides a clear framework for Buddhists to live by but how Buddhists choose to live is also very important

Useful Words

Abhidhamma basket, ascetic, canon, Pali, Sanskrit, sutta/sutra, Sutta basket, Tipitaka, Vinaya basket

Skills practised

- Literacy: using key terms from another language with confidence
- Communication: trying to pass on a message correctly by word of mouth
- Interpretation: explaining how and why Buddhists use scripture
- Evaluation: considering how important scripture is to Buddhists and why people find guidelines in life useful
- Application: scripting a discussion to explore a range of characters' guidelines for living
- Reflection: considering the sources of authority in their own lives and the nature of religious wisdom and life experience

Resources

- 2.1 Baskets Worksheet: students must explain aspects of the Tipitaka and investigate teachings
- 2.1 Scripture Interactive Activity: students test their understanding of the structure and languages of Buddhist scripture
- 2.1 Lesson Player: a ready-to-go presentation with built-in resources and teacher notes
- 2 Image Gallery: a useful gallery of photos and illustrations from the chapter
- 2.1 Self-Assessment Sheet: students evaluate their learning against the lesson objectives

Ideas for starters

1. Use the first starter from the *Student Book*. Encourage students to discuss as a class what is meant by the term 'authority' while you write their ideas on the board. Ask students what conclusions they can draw from this. Share and compare the sources of authority in their own lives.

2. Facilitate a class game of Chinese Whispers. (The classic is 'Send reinforcements, we're going to advance'.) Then compare the original and the final message. Draw out how carefully people have to listen to messages and stories when they cannot write them down. Explain that the Buddha lived when most people did not often read or write, so his teachings were passed on by word of mouth, i.e. the oral tradition. You could also briefly consider what might make religious stories memorable.

Activity guidance

- Discuss Activity **1** in the *Student Book* and then ask students to start their own Sutta Pitaka (basket of teachings). Suggest that they copy short Buddhist teachings that appeal to them into their exercise book as they come across them in the *Student Book* and in their own research.

- Activity **2** in the *Student Book* asks students to make a decorated bookmark to explain why scripture is important to Buddhists and how it is used. Encourage them to spend most of their time thinking about how to explain the importance and use of scripture.

- Activity **3** in the *Student Book* asks students to make notes on a conversation between various characters in order to explore guidelines for living. Divide them into groups of three and let each group allocate the three roles. Allow time for the groups to role-play and make notes on their conclusions. Encourage students to feed back about what they have discovered through this activity.

Ideas for plenaries

1. Ask students to suggest, one at a time, one word to complete a sentence that summarizes the lesson.

2. Ask students to write a paragraph, or present their views in another way, on what they have learned in the lesson.

Further class and homework activities

1. Ask students to find out what the Heart Sutra and Diamond Sutra are about.

2. 2.1 Baskets Worksheet on the *Buddhism Kerboodle* could work well as a plenary or homework activity.

3. 2.1 Scripture Interactive Activity on the *Buddhism Kerboodle*.

4. Further suggestions on page 46 of this book.

2.2 How can Stories Inspire?

The unit in brief

This unit introduces students to the Jataka Tales and the story of the Monkey King in particular. It gives them the opportunity to reflect on the importance of stories in teaching about moral choices.

Key ideas

- Stories can be a good way of getting a point across
- Some stories have a deeper meaning or moral
- The Jataka Tales tell stories about the previous lives of the Buddha
- A good ruler sacrifices himself for his people

Skills practised

- Literacy: reading independently and writing an inscription
- Interpretation: explaining the moral in a story
- Evaluation: considering how good stories are at teaching about moral choices
- Enquiry: researching other Jataka Tales
- Communication: creating a cartoon that tells a moral story
- Reflection: considering how they could use a Jataka Tale to develop their character

Resources

- 2.2 Monkey King Audio Clip: a reading of the tale of The Monkey King and the Mangoes

- 2.2 Monument Worksheet: students design a monument to the Money King

- 2.2 Jataka Tales Interactive Activity: students complete the gaps in a paragraph summarizing the nature and purpose of the Jataka Tales

- 2.2 Lesson Player: a ready-to-go presentation with built-in resources and teacher notes

- 2 Image Gallery: a useful gallery of photos and illustrations from the chapter

- 2.2 Self-Assessment Sheet: students evaluate their learning against the lesson objectives

Ideas for starters

1. Use the starters in the *Student Book* to start class discussion. Remind students of fairy stories with similar themes (innocent young heroines, wicked witches, dashing rescuers) and fables such as those of Aesop, Br'er Rabbit and the Anansi stories. Draw out that stories like this are favourites with young children, who remember the story and absorb the moral without realizing.

2. You could start the lesson by telling a short moral story. Then ask students to identify the moral and what makes it

memorable. Follow up with the second starter question in the *Student Book*.

3. Ask the first starter question in the *Student Book*. Ask students to tell their favourite story to a partner or the class.

Activity guidance

- Read the story of the Monkey King to the class or ask students to read it independently. For Activity **1** in the *Student Book*, ask pairs to share their questions with the class. Vote on which three questions they want to explore together.

- Remind students that their cartoon for Activity **2** in the *Student Book* should have a clear moral. Ask them to hand in a note with their moral written on it. Later, number all the cartoons and display them on the wall. Explain that before the next lesson, students should write what they think the moral of each cartoon is. In the next lesson, read out each moral and score each cartoon with the number of correct guesses. The cartoon with the most correct guesses wins.

- Invite one or two students to read out their inscriptions for Activity **3** in the *Student Book*. The class should then ask them questions on their reasons for using certain words and decorations.

Ideas for plenaries

1. Ask students to choose a good quality that they admire in one of the characters they have found out about. They should say why they would like to develop that quality in themselves and how they might go about doing that.

2. Discuss with the students the idea that telling stories is a universal human characteristic. Do they agree? Why do they think people keep telling and passing on stories?

Further class and homework activities

1. Ask students to research other Jataka Tales. They should choose one, write the story in their own words, and then add a paragraph explaining the moral.

2. You could use 2.2 Monument Worksheet on the *Buddhism Kerboodle* as a way of encouraging students to consider the moral qualities of the Monkey King.

3. Ask students to research other 'inspiring stories' from the scripture of other faiths. For examples, see Chapter 2 in the *Christianity Student Book*, or Chapter 2 in the *Hinduism Student Book*.

4. 2.2 Jataka Tales Interactive Activity on the *Buddhism Kerboodle*.

5. Further suggestions on page 46 of this book.

2.3 Which is the Right Path?

The unit in brief

This unit introduces students to the Noble Eightfold Path, explaining how it works as a guide for living and how it came to be one of the Buddha's central teachings. It encourages students to consider its importance to Buddhists and its relevance in the modern world.

Key ideas

- The Buddha found Enlightenment by following the Middle Way, which he taught was how to escape from the endless cycle of birth and rebirth
- Escape from the cycle leads to Nibbana, the state of perfect peace
- The Buddha's teaching about the Middle Way is outlined in the Noble Eightfold Path – a guide for living in the right way with the right attitudes

Useful Words

Nibbana/Nirvana, Noble Eightfold Path

Skills practised

- Evaluation: considering how to know right from wrong and the value of the Noble Eightfold Path
- Application: considering how the Noble Eightfold Path would help with guidelines for school life
- Research: finding out how Buddhists try to live according to the Buddha's teachings
- Reflection: considering the concept of a world without suffering

Resources

- 2.3 Right Path Film Clip: Molly explains how she tries to follow the Noble Eightfold Path in everyday life
- 2.3 Film Worksheet: students assess their understanding of the case study film clips by linking ideas to the *Student Book*
- 2.3 Eightfold Path Interactive Activity: students consider whether certain actions would be acceptable to a Buddhist following the Noble Eightfold Path
- 2.3 Lesson Player: a ready-to-go presentation with built-in resources and teacher notes
- 2 Image Gallery: a useful gallery of photos and illustrations from the chapter
- 2.3 Self-Assessment Sheet: students evaluate their learning against the lesson objectives

Ideas for starters

1. Use the starter from the *Student Book*. Allow students two minutes to write a response to the question. Share opinions and come to a consensus as a class.

2. Ask students to produce a mind-map about sources of authority and judgement. You could prompt them with sources such as parents, teachers, religion, government, and laws.

3. As a class, discuss what age children can be relied upon to know right from wrong and to take responsibility for their own decisions.

Activity guidance

- For Activity **1** in the *Student Book*, you could divide students into eight groups so that each group considers one aspect of the Noble Eightfold Path. Each group should agree on one guideline for living in the school community based on their part of the Noble Eightfold Path. Share the guidelines as a class. You could extend the activity so that students create decorated posters of their guidelines and then nominate a day or a week in which the whole class tries their best to follow the guidelines. Discuss how easy or difficult it was afterwards.

Ideas for plenaries

1. Use the Reflection from the *Student Book*.

2. Ask students to rank the eight components of the Eightfold Path in order of importance to them.

3. Ask students to make a bookmark for Molly to give her tips on following Right Speech.

4. Ask students to compile their own list of eight guidelines for life that they think would lead to freedom from suffering.

5. Ask students to write five versions of the following sentence by filling in the blanks: 'Because I believe… , I behave like this:… .' You could write an example of your own on the board to get them started.

Further class and homework activities

1. Students could learn the eight points of the Noble Eightfold Path for a quick test next lesson.

2. 2.3 Film Worksheet on the *Buddhism Kerboodle*.

3. 2.3 Eightfold Path Interactive Activity on the *Buddhism Kerboodle*.

4. Further suggestions on page 46 of this book.

2.4 The Five Precepts

The unit in brief

In introducing the Five Precepts, this unit focuses on ethics and the moral codes valued by Buddhists. It gives students the opportunity to consider what they value as good characteristics.

Key ideas

- Buddhists follow ethical codes, which give guidelines on how to think and act
- Lay Buddhists try to live by the Five Precepts, which focus on avoiding negative actions and developing positive ones
- Buddhists believe that positive actions create positive kamma

Skills practised

- Interpretation: explaining the Five Precepts and their relevance to modern life
- Reflection: considering their own qualities and those that they would like to develop
- Evaluation: ranking the Five Precepts in order of personal importance
- Problem-solving: considering the difficulties of following the Five Precepts and ways to overcome them
- Application: role-playing to explore the Five Precepts
- Literacy: writing a short story or comic strip

Resources

- 2.4 Precepts Film Clip: Tom discusses how he relates to the Five Precepts
- 2.4 Film Worksheet: students assess their understanding of the case study film clips by linking ideas to the *Student Book*
- 2.4 Guidelines Interactive Activity: students assess their knowledge about the ethical guidelines by which Buddhists live their lives
- 2.4 Lesson Player: a ready-to-go presentation with built-in resources and teacher notes
- 2 Image Gallery: a useful gallery of photos and illustrations from the chapter
- 2.4 Self-Assessment Sheet: students evaluate their learning against the lesson objectives

Ideas for starters

1. Ask students to create an agreed set of five guidelines for life in class. You could use a voting system. Challenge the class to keep to the guidelines for a week and then discuss how difficult they were to keep at the start of another lesson. Display the guidelines in class as a reminder.

2. Use the starter in the *Student Book* with care and sensitivity.

Activity guidance

- Activity **1** in the *Student Book* could form the basis of a class discussion, followed by a vote. Ask them to write down their immediate response to the outcome. If they do not agree, why not?

- The role-plays for Activity **2** in the *Student Book* could show someone being presented with the opportunity to perform one of the negative actions and instead choosing to take the positive action. Ask groups to perform their role-play. Invite the rest of the students to put up their hands to stop the action at any point and ask what the characters are thinking.

- Invite students to share their stories or comic strips for Activity **3** in the *Student Book*.

- Invite students to share their list of guidelines for Activity **4** in the *Student Book*.

Ideas for plenaries

1. Use the Reflection from the *Student Book*. Ask: do you think it becomes easier or more difficult to change as you get older? Why?

2. Display the text of each of the Five Precepts on separate sheets of paper around the room. Ask students to stand in front of the Precept they think is most important. Count the number of students for each Precept and discuss the results as a class.

3. Ask students to learn the Five Precepts for a quick test next lesson.

Further class and homework activities

1. 2.4 Film Worksheet on the *Buddhism Kerboodle*.

2. 2.4 Guidelines Interactive Activity on the *Buddhism Kerboodle*.

3. Further suggestions on page 46 of this book.

2.5 Let's Celebrate!

The unit in brief

This unit gives students the opportunity to reflect on why celebrations are important and what makes them so. It introduces the Buddhist festival of Wesak and the importance of a sense of community to Buddhists.

Key ideas

- Many Buddhists celebrate Wesak in memory of the Buddha's birth, Enlightenment and death
- Many Buddhists visit temples and monasteries to pay respect to the Buddha and hear teachings
- Celebrations like this help to give Buddhists a sense of belonging to a community

Useful Words

Buddharupa, Wesak

Skills practised

- Analysis: comparing festivals from different faiths
- Literacy: writing an explanation of their own views
- Communication: designing a card and planning events for Wesak celebrations
- Reflection: considering the importance of celebrations

Resources

- 2.5 Wesak Film Clip: Mrs Harvey explains what happens at Wesak and what she likes about it
- 2.5 Film Worksheet: students assess their understanding of the case study film clips by linking ideas to the *Student Book*
- 2.5 Festival Interactive Activity: students show their knowledge about the most widely celebrated festival in the Buddhist calendar
- 2.5 Lesson Player: a ready-to-go presentation with built-in resources and teacher notes
- 2 Image Gallery: a useful gallery of photos and illustrations from the chapter
- 2.5 Self-Assessment Sheet: students evaluate their learning against the lesson objectives

Ideas for starters

1. Display the picture of the Wesak celebration in the *Student Book* as students enter the room. Ask: why is it good to celebrate?

2. Ask students to discuss the first starter in the *Student Book* in pairs. As a class, share the things necessary for a successful party. Draw out that a sense of belonging and perhaps certain customs are important.

3. Use the second starter from the *Student Book* to stimulate a brief discussion on which events students celebrate. What non-religious events worth celebrating can they think of?

4. Ask students which festivals they know from other faiths they have studied.

Activity guidance

- Extend Activity **1** in the *Student Book* by organizing students into small groups, and nominating one student in each group to take the 'hot-seat' as Mrs Harvey. They should answer others' questions.

- For Activity **2** in the *Student Book*, students could compile a grid to compare the festivals. Prompt them with categories: What does the festival celebrate? When is it? What are the customs? What special symbols are used? For more on festivals of other faiths, see Unit 3.2 in the *Judaism Student Book* or Chapter 3 in the *Islam Student Book*.

- As an alternative to writing a response for Activity **3** in the *Student Book*, you could organize a debate on the statement. Remind students to be respectful of each others' views, and take a final vote.

- After completing Activity **4** of the *Student Book*, ask students to present their proposals to the class. Take a vote on the best ideas. If possible, hold a Wesak Day celebration incorporating as many of the planned elements as is practical.

Ideas for plenaries

1. Use the Reflection from the *Student Book*, drawing out their reasons.

2. Nominate students to tell the class which their favourite celebration or religious festival is, and why.

3. If you chose to complete Activity **3** in the *Student Book* as a debate, ask students if they agree with the outcome. If not, they should explain why.

4. Ask students to summarize in one sentence the significance of light in the celebration of Wesak.

Further class and homework activities

1. Ask students to find out about other Buddhist festivals and discover where and how they are celebrated.

2. Ask students to make a decorative poster advertising the celebrations for Wesak Day at a Buddhist temple.

3. 2.5 Film Worksheet on the *Buddhism Kerboodle*.

4. 2.5 Festival Interactive Activity on the *Buddhism Kerboodle*.

5. Further suggestions on page 46 of this book.

2.6 Life and Death: The Never-Ending Circle

The unit in brief

This unit gives more detail about Buddhist beliefs around life and death. It explains the concepts of rebirth, samsara and the six realms, as represented by the Bhavacakka (Wheel of Life). Students are encouraged to reflect on their own beliefs about what happens after death.

Key ideas

- Buddhists believe that life is an endless cycle of birth and rebirth called samsara
- A person is reborn into one of six realms, represented by the Bhavacakka (Wheel of Life)
- Some realms seem to be more pleasant than others, although dukkha exists in all of them
- Buddhists can only end samsara and reach Nibbana through Enlightenment
- The Buddha reached Enlightenment in his lifetime but chose to stay and teach
- Buddhists celebrate the Buddha's death on Nibbana Day

Useful Words

Bhavacakka, Nibbana Day, samsara

Skills practised

- Interpretation: explaining Buddhist beliefs about life, death and rebirth
- Reflection: considering the impermanence of life and their own beliefs about life and death
- Communication: representing the universe symbolically as a wheel
- Literacy: writing an obituary for the Buddha
- Analysis: comparing the beliefs of various faiths about life and death

Resources

- 📄 2.6 Biography Worksheet: students create a mini-biography for the Buddha
- ⬉ 2.6 Life and Death Interactive Activity: students must match key terms from the unit to the correct definition
- 🎓 2.6 Lesson Player: a ready-to-go presentation with built-in resources and teacher notes
- 🖥 2 Image Gallery: a useful gallery of photos and illustrations from the chapter
- 📄 2.6 Self-Assessment Sheet: students evaluate their learning against the lesson objectives

Ideas for starters

1. Display the picture of the Bhavacakka (Wheel of Life) in the *Student Book* as students enter the room. Spend a few minutes exploring what they can see in it.

Living Faiths Buddhism

2. Use the first starter in the *Student Book*. Encourage students to explain their views.

3. Use the second starter in the *Student Book* as the basis of a class discussion. If students are unsure of what they think, ask them to recall the beliefs of other faiths they have studied.

4. Write the words 'Rebirth', 'Heaven' and 'Hell' on the board. Ask students what they think of in connection with each word. What do they think are the good and bad points about each concept?

Activity guidance

- You could make available a collection of images of Bhavacakka as inspiration for Activity **1** in the *Student Book*. If time is short, students could make a plan for the wheel, subdividing the circle and writing notes on what images they will use. They could discuss their plans with a partner to decide on improvements, and finish their design for homework.

- In preparation for Activity **2** in the *Student Book*, show students a small selection of real biographies and identify the important features.

Ideas for plenaries

1. Use the Reflection from the *Student Book*.

2. Ask students to revisit their responses to starter **4** above. Ask if they have changed their ideas about any of the words and if so, why.

3. Display the designs from Activity **1** in the *Student Book*. Take a vote on which is the best symbolic representation of the universe.

4. Ask students to read out their obituaries from Activity **2** in the *Student Book*. Ask students to discuss how well they celebrate the Buddha's life. Invite comments on two positive points and one area to improve on.

Further class and homework activities

1. Ask students to write a short essay based on the Reflection in the *Student Book* for homework.

2. Ask students to research how Nibbana Day is celebrated around the world.

3. You could use 2.6 Biography Worksheet on the *Buddhism Kerboodle* at the end of the lesson to help students demonstrate their knowledge of the Buddha's teachings on samsara and Nibbana.

4. 2.6 Life and Death Interactive Activity on the *Buddhism Kerboodle*.

5. Further suggestions on page 46 of this book.

2.7 Can You Worship Without a God?

The unit in brief

This unit encourages students to explore what worship means in general and to Buddhists in particular. It explains different forms of Buddhist worship and the symbolism of different offerings. It also prompts students to consider whether worship is possible without a god.

Key ideas

- Worship is showing respect to someone or something
- Buddhists do not believe in a god
- Buddhist worship takes many forms, including chanting, making offerings, listening to scripture and meditation, and can be done in a temple or at home
- Different offerings have symbolic significance
- There is no special architectural style for temples

Useful Words

anjali mudda, mantra, prostration, puja, Sangha

Skills practised

- Interpretation: explaining what worship means
- Enquiry: exploring different types of Buddhist worship
- Communication: producing a guide to Buddhist worship
- Analysis: considering whether worship without a god is possible
- Reflection: considering whether it is possible to be spiritual without being religious
- Evaluation: giving a personal response to chanting

Resources

- 2.7 Worship Film Clip A: Boonyoung explains why worshipping as part of the Sangha is important
- 2.7 Worship Film Clip B: the Aldam family discusses their personal approach to worship
- 2.7 Film Worksheet: students assess their understanding of the case study film clips by linking ideas to the *Student Book*
- 2.7 True or False Interactive Activity: students decide whether statements about Buddhist worship are true or false
- 2.7 Lesson Player: a ready-to-go presentation with built-in resources and teacher notes
- 2 Image Gallery: a useful gallery of photos and illustrations from the chapter
- 2.7 Self-Assessment Sheet: students evaluate their learning against the lesson objectives

Ideas for starters

1. Use the starters in the *Student Book* to stimulate discussion.

2. Demonstrate the anjali mudda gesture (hands together as in prayer). Ask: what does this gesture mean? What feelings do you associate with it? In which other religions or cultures is it used?

3. Write the word 'worship' on the board and ask students for ten words they associate with it. What examples of worship can they think of?

Activity guidance

- Students could produce the text for the guide in Activity **1** of the *Student Book* in the lesson and then illustrate it for homework. They could draw images or download them from the Internet.

- As an alternative to a written response for Activity **2** in the *Student Book*, use the statement as a basis for discussion. You could extend the discussion to consider whether, without a belief in a god, Buddhism is actually a religion.

- Ask students to close their eyes and sit quietly in preparation for Activity **3** of the *Student Book*. Play some Buddhist chanting (you could use 3.3 Chant Audio Clip). Ask students to write three to five words on the board or on sticky notes, without consulting others, to describe how the chanting makes them feel. Compare and discuss their impressions.

Ideas for plenaries

1. Use the Reflection from the *Student Book*. Make sure students understand the meaning of 'spiritual' in this context.

2. Ask students to say whether they find certain elements of Buddhist worship appealing, and why or why not.

3. As a class, create a Venn diagram on the board showing the similarities and differences between Buddhist worship and that of one or two other faiths they have studied. It might be easiest to start with the features of Buddhist worship and then add the others.

Further class and homework activities

1. Ask students to write a short paragraph starting 'Buddhists worship because...'.

2. 2.7 Film Worksheet on the *Buddhism Kerboodle*.

3. 2.7 True or False Interactive Activity on the *Buddhism Kerboodle*.

4. Further suggestions on page 46 of this book.

Chapter 2 Further Suggestions

These suggestions are addressed directly to students.

2.1 Read All About It!

1 Create a poster that shows all of the sources of authority in your life. *

2 'We all need authority in our lives.' Do you agree with this statement? Explain why or why not. **

3 What do we mean by 'authority'? Share your thoughts as a blog, poem, song or picture. **

4 Organize a large group of friends to spend a whole day following all the school rules, e.g. perfect uniform, no gum, moving quietly in the corridors, hands up, listening, etc. Present your reflections to the class. Did you know all the rules? How hard was it to follow them? Did anyone notice you behaving differently? **

2.2 How can Stories Inspire?

1 Reread the story of the Monkey King. Write your own story in the style of a Jataka Tale. It must have a clear moral that encourages people to live and behave in a way that Buddhists would consider to be better. ***

2 Choose one story from the Jataka Tales and draw a picture based on it. You could focus on one particular aspect or try to represent the whole story. **

3 'Stories are powerful.' Write a response to this statement, using examples from the Jataka Tales. ***

2.3 Which is the Right Path?

1 Find out more about the Buddhist concept of Nibbana. Is there a similar belief in other faiths you have studied? **

2 'Life would be better if everyone followed the Noble Eightfold Path.' Do you agree with this statement? Explain your answer. **

3 What do you think the Buddha would say about the modern world? Would he offer the same teachings as he did when he was alive or would he change them? Explain your views. ***

2.4 The Five Precepts

1a Write a definition of a moral code. **

 b Explain, with reference to your definition, how the Five Precepts are a moral code. ***

2 Make a mind-map to show where your moral code has come from. *

3 Design a poster for a Buddhist community centre to show what the Five Precepts are and why they are important. **

2.5 Let's Celebrate!

1 Find out more about how Wesak is celebrated around the world. Make notes about the customs that people in different countries have for celebrating it. **

2 'Celebrating special events encourages people in their faith.' Do you think that this statement is true or false? Why? There is no correct answer, so consider your opinions. You may wish to include the opinions of others. **

3 Compare how Buddhists celebrate Wesak with celebrations that mark memorable dates in the lives of central figures from other faiths you have studied. What are the similarities and differences? ***

2.6 Life and Death: The Never-Ending Circle

1 Find more pictures of the Bhavacakka. Are there any differences between the pictures? What do you think might be the reason for any differences? *

2 Research some of the teachings the Buddha gave just before he died. *

3 'Death is not the end.' Respond to this statement, using your own views and the beliefs of faiths you have studied. ***

4 Make an invitation asking people to attend your Nibbana Day celebrations. Tell them what to expect and what to bring. **

5 Explore accounts of rebirth from around the world and evaluate how believable they are. ***

2.7 Can You Worship Without a God?

1 Make a tally chart over two weeks of the number of celebrities you see on television and in magazines using the anjali mudda gesture. Why do you think they use it? *

2 Find out about Buddhist places of worship around the world. What similarities and differences do they have? **

3 Compare Buddhist forms and places of worship with those in other faiths you have studied. ***

4 Compare the Buddha with central figures in other faiths you have studied. What are the similarities and differences? ***

Chapter 2 Assessment

Assessment in the *Student Book*

You will find an assessment task at the end of every chapter that focuses on AT2. In this chapter, the task asks students to design and market an ethical product, based on Buddhists teachings on ethics.

In the *Student Book* (and on the supporting worksheets), you'll find guidance about levels of assessment that you can use to help your students understand what their work should include. You could ask them to use these criteria for self- or peer-assessment once they've completed the task.

Assessment Task for Chapter 2 (pages **36–37** of the *Buddhism Student Book*)

Objectives

- Identify the features of a product that fits in with the teachings of the Buddha
- Make clear reference to the Noble Eightfold Path and the Five Precepts
- Explain why Buddhists would approve of the product

Task

You have been approached by an ethical company that wants to make a product that will appeal to Buddhist purchasers.

a Decide on the product. It must do no harm to living things or the environment, in use or the way it's made, and must also take into account the Noble Eightfold Path and the Five Precepts. Be prepared to justify your choice with reference to Buddhist teachings.

b Design a marketing booklet that will accompany the product in which you explain clearly, using the Noble Eightfold Path and the Five Precepts, why it will appeal to Buddhists.

Assessment in *Kerboodle*

On the *Buddhism Kerboodle*, you'll find resources to use when introducing the assessment task to the class.

You can use the *Chapter 2 Assessment Task Presentation* as a front-of-class tool to help your students unpack the assessment criteria, and understand what is expected of them.

Chapter 2 Assessment Worksheets accompany the task, so that once you finish the presentation, your students can easily get started.

Auto-marked tests

The *Buddhism Kerboodle* also contains auto-marked tests for each chapter to help save you time setting questions and marking for AT1. The test for this chapter contains 15 questions and will take most students about half an hour. Test results are automatically stored in the markbook.

Digital markbook

A markbook and a reporting function complete the *Kerboodle* assessment package, so you can keep all your students' test results and assessment scores in one place. This can include the auto-marked tests as well as pieces of work you or the students have marked by hand.

▲   Assessment resources for Chapter 2 on the *Buddhism Kerboodle*

Chapter 3 Overview
Belonging to the Buddhist Faith

Helping you deliver Key Stage 3 RE

This chapter addresses the following areas of the Programme of Study:

Key concepts

Practices and ways of life
- Explore the impact of religions and beliefs on how people live their lives

Expressing meaning
- Appreciate that individuals and cultures express their beliefs and values through many different forms

Key processes

Learning about religion
- Apply a wide range of religious and philosophical vocabulary consistently and accurately, recognizing both the power and limitations of language in expressing religious ideas and beliefs

Learning from religion
- Express insights into the significance and value of religion and other world views for personal, local and global human relationships

The big picture

These are the key ideas behind this chapter:

- Community is very important to Buddhists.
- There are many different schools of Buddhism, which have different practices.
- Some Buddhists choose to live a monastic life.
- Meditation is used to find calm and clarity of thought.
- Zen Buddhism teaches that Enlightenment is within everyone.
- Happiness can be taught and learned.

Chapter outline

Use this to give students a mental roadmap for the chapter:

3.1 What does it Mean to Belong? – explores the importance of community to Buddhists and explains how the ordained and lay Buddhist communities interact; includes a case study

3.2 Same Faith, Different Ways – introduces Mahayana and Theravada Buddhism, and explores whether variety is a good thing; includes a case study

3.3 Special Feature: Let's Meet a Monk – presents the case study of a Theravada monk who lives in a temple in Birmingham

3.4 Uncluttering Your Mind – explores meditation in more detail and explains how it is practised in a variety of different ways; includes a case study

3.5 The Sound of One Hand Clapping – introduces Zen Buddhism, meditation and the idea of living in the moment

3.6 The Happiest Man in the World? – looks at the life and work of Matthieu Ricard, the Dalai Lama's French translator, who is named by some scientists as the happiest man in the world

Opportunities for assessment

Summative assessments on the *Buddhism Kerboodle* include auto-marked tests, interactive activities and self-assessment worksheets.

The end-of-chapter assessment task in the *Student Book* provides formative assessment. Supporting materials for the assessment task can be found on the *Buddhism Kerboodle*, such as the Assessment Task Presentation and related worksheets.

There are other opportunities for assessment too. For example, you could use some of the activities or reflection points throughout each *Student Book* unit, or some of the 'Further suggestions' at the end of this chapter.

Getting ready for this chapter

- Spend some time researching different schools of Buddhism, their practices and celebrations, to be ready for students' questions.
- Read through the chapter and familiarize yourself with the activities so that you can set up the classroom ready for each lesson. For example, you could display pictures from Units 3.1, 3.3 and 3.4 as students enter the room to start discussion.
- It is worth practising some chanting and meditation alone at home before encouraging students to participate in it in Units 3.3 and 3.4. The more comfortable you are, the better the learning experience. Alternatively, arrange for a practitioner to come in and take a special lesson.

- Familiarize yourself with Matthieu Ricard's official website so that you can encourage in-depth discussion in Unit 3.6.

Objectives and outcomes for this chapter

Objectives	Unit	Outcomes
Most students will:		Most students will be able to:
• define the importance of community to Buddhists • explore the place of religious communities in society • reflect on the different roles people play in a community.	3.1	• explain how and why community is important to Buddhists • describe and explain the place of religious communities in society • evaluate the fact that people play different roles in a community.
• identify examples of diversity in Buddhist belief and practice • explain how Buddhists from different traditions aim for the same goal • reflect on whether unity can be found despite differences in practice.	3.2	• describe the differences between Mahayana and Theravada Buddhism • use key terms to explain how a Buddhist belief can help unite people • express their own ideas on when variety is a good thing and when it may cause conflict.
• identify why people become Buddhist monks and nuns • explore and evaluate the life of a Theravada Buddhist monk • reflect on the idea of committing their life to a community.	3.3	• consider why some people become Buddhist monks or nuns • describe the life of a Theravada Buddhist monk, based on a case study • give an opinion on what it would feel like to commit their life to a community.
• explore the importance of meditation to Buddhists • analyse different meditation styles • reflect on the experience of meditation.	3.4	• explain the purpose and importance of meditation to Buddhists • compare and evaluate different styles of meditation • express how they feel about meditation.
• identify some of the beliefs and practices of Zen Buddhists • analyse how Zen practices differ from other types of Buddhism • reflect on what it means to 'live in the moment'.	3.5	• describe what Zen Buddhists believe about Enlightenment and the different ways they meditate • analyse how Zen practices are different from other types of Buddhism • evaluate how easy it is to live in the moment and how the practice could change their life.
• explore the link between meditation and happiness • investigate the life of Matthieu Ricard • reflect on the nature of happiness.	3.6	• explain the possible links between meditation and happiness • describe and evaluate the life of Matthieu Ricard • say what makes them happy and give an opinion on whether happiness comes from within or from external sources.

3.1 What does it Mean to Belong?

The unit in brief

This unit explains the importance of community to Buddhists and how the monastic and lay communities interact. It introduces the way monks and nuns live, and how they are supported by the lay community.

Key ideas

- The Buddha taught that friends and community are very important
- The wider community of Buddhists is called the Sangha.
- The Buddha, the dhamma and the Sangha are known as the Three Refuges
- Buddhist monks and nuns live a simple life, following over 250 vows and providing teaching in monasteries
- Non-ordained Buddhists keep the Five Precepts and support the monks and nuns

Useful Words

bhikkhu, bhikkhuni, ordained, Three Refuges/Three Jewels, upsaka

Skills practised

- Thinking: reflecting on what 'community' means and the communities they belong to
- Reflection: considering which rules they would find most difficult to keep
- Literacy: writing a story or cartoon based on friendship
- Enquiry: preparing questions to ask a Buddhist about her relationship with ordained Buddhists

Resources

- 3.1 Community Film Clip: Mrs Harvey explains what she gains from being part of a Buddhist community
- 3.1 Film Worksheet: students assess their understanding of the case study film clips by linking ideas to the *Student Book*
- 3.1 Sangha Interactive Activity: students complete sentences about the concept of community in Buddhism
- 3.1 Lesson Player: a ready-to-go presentation with built-in resources and teacher notes
- 3 Image Gallery: a useful gallery of photos and illustrations from the chapter
- 3.1 Self-Assessment Sheet: students evaluate their learning against the lesson objectives

Ideas for starters

1. Display the picture of the rock concert crowd as students enter the room. Use the first starter question and/or the picture caption in the *Student Book* to stimulate discussion.

2. Ask students to take turns sitting in the teacher's chair at the front of the class. Give them ten seconds each to say what comes to mind when they hear the word 'community'. Write all the ideas on the board.

3. Ask students to work in pairs to produce mind-maps of what 'community' means to them and which communities they belong to.

4. Use the second starter in the *Student Book*, giving students three minutes to draw images that come to mind when they think of monks and nuns. They could review these at the end of the lesson.

Activity guidance

*   Recap the Five Precepts (see Unit 2.4) in preparation for Activity **1** in the *Student Book*. Ask students to discuss the questions in pairs and then open up the topic to class discussion.

*   Extend Activity **3** in the *Student Book* by getting students to ask 'Mrs Harvey' the questions they have prepared. You could take the role yourself or ask a student or member of the local Buddhist community to participate.

*   To help make interfaith links, you could compare Buddhist views with Christian responses to community in Unit 3.2 of the *Christianity Student Book*.

Ideas for plenaries

1. Use the Reflection from the *Student Book*. Give students three minutes to write an independent response. Ask volunteers to read their responses.

2. Ask students to read the stories or explain the cartoons they created in Activity **2** in the *Student Book* to the class.

Further class and homework activities

1. Ask students to make a collage of all the different communities they belong to. They could write captions to explain why each community is important to them.

2. Ask students to research some of the vows that Buddhist monks and nuns have to keep.

3. 'Life as a Buddhist monk or nun is impossible to stick to strictly.' Ask students to write a response to this statement.

4. 3.1 Film Worksheet on the *Buddhism Kerboodle*.

5. 3.1 Sangha Interactive Activity on the *Buddhism Kerboodle*.

6. Further suggestions on page 62 of this book.

3.2 Same Faith, Different Ways

The unit in brief

This unit introduces the idea that there are many types of Buddhism. It explains some of the differences and similarities between the two main schools – Mahayana and Theravada Buddhism. It explores whether differences hinder unity and whether variety is a good thing.

Key ideas

- There are different schools of Buddhism and a wide range of ways of practising the faith
- The two main schools/traditions are Mahayana and Theravada Buddhism
- The original teaching of the Buddha, a simple life of meditation and the monastic life are important to Theravada Buddhists
- Mahayana Buddhism has spread more widely and has been adapted to many different cultures

Useful Words

bodhisattva, Mahayana, Theravada

Skills practised

- Thinking: reflecting on differences and similarities in music and religion
- Analysis: suggesting how a Buddhist belief helps to unite people and whether there is more in Buddhism that unites than divides
- Enquiry: finding out about the work of a Buddhist centre
- Literacy: writing a newspaper article
- Reflection: considering whether variety in life is a good thing

Resources

- 3.2 Mahayana Film Clip: The Aldam family discusses their involvement in the Jamyang Buddhist Centre

- 3.2 Film Worksheet: students assess their understanding of the case study film clips by linking ideas to the *Student Book*

- 3.2 Bodhisattva Audio Clip: the story of the bodhisattva, Avalokiteśvara, famous for his compassion

- 3.2 Traditions Interactive Activity: students categorize statements as referring to either the Theravada or the Mahayana School of Buddhism

- 3.2 Lesson Player: a ready-to-go presentation with built-in resources and teacher notes

- 3 Image Gallery: a useful gallery of photos and illustrations from the chapter

- 3.2 Self-Assessment Sheet: students evaluate their learning against the lesson objectives

Ideas for starters

1. Use the starter in the *Student Book*.
2. Ask students to work in pairs to list five things that cause disunity. Ask them to swap their lists with another pair and suggest solutions to the problems.

3. Show students headlines and cuttings from news articles about conflict and disunity around the world. Discuss ways to find possible solutions. Draw out that honest communication and finding common aims are often a good way to start trying to solve disputes.

4. Ask students to list different branches of Christianity and then ask what they have in common. Explain that Buddhism is structured in a similar way.

Activity guidance

- For Activity **1** in the *Student Book*, encourage students to think of the Five Precepts and the Noble Eightfold Path.

- Students need to write about a Buddhist centre for Activity **3** in the *Student Book*. You can locate centres anywhere in the UK by county (or in the world) using the World Buddhist Directory online. You might then be able to organize a visit. Students could write research notes in class and complete their articles for homework. The articles could be read and displayed in class or posted on the school website.

Ideas for plenaries

1. Use the Reflection from the *Student Book*, asking students to take turns to give their thoughts.

2. Ask students to work in pairs to challenge each other to give clear and accurate definitions of Theravada Buddhism, Mahayana Buddhism and bodhisattva. Share and agree class definitions.

3. Ask students to write two or three sentences starting with 'Today I have learned...'. Share a few responses.

4. As a class, compile two lists on the board of things that divide the school community and things that unite it. Which things do students think have the biggest impact? Can they suggest any solutions to the things that divide?

Further class and homework activities

1. Ask students to collect headings and cuttings from news articles about disputes and conflict around the world over one or two weeks. They can then make a class collage of their cuttings linked to a large world map. Ask them to plan where they would go on a peace pilgrimage in an attempt to end conflict. They must plan the route and be able to justify their choices.

2. 3.2 Film Worksheet on the *Buddhism Kerboodle*.

3. 3.2 Traditions Interactive Activity on the *Buddhism Kerboodle*.

4. Further suggestions on page 62 of this book.

3.3 Special Feature: Let's Meet a Monk

The unit in brief

This unit presents a case study of Phra Aod Boonyoung, a Theravada monk from a temple in Birmingham. It explains how people become Buddhist monks, aspects of Boonyoung's daily routine and work, and how he feels about being a monk in Birmingham.

Key ideas

- Monks are given their Buddhist names when they are ordained
- There are over 500 Buddhist groups and centres in Britain
- The monks pay respect to the Buddha, follow the dhamma, meditate and chant; they also teach meditation and share the teachings with lay people
- Novice monks need to follow the precepts, practise meditation and read the scriptures

Skills practised

- Reflection: considering their own life ambitions
- Communication: creating a poster to explain the life, duties and experiences of a Buddhist monk
- Enquiry: finding out about the life of a Buddhist monk by asking questions
- Literacy: writing diary entries about monastic life

Resources

- 3.3 Monk Film Clip A: Boonyoung discusses his life as a monk; part 1 of 3
- 3.3 Monk Film Clip B: Boonyoung discusses his life as a monk; part 2 of 3
- 3.3 Monk Film Clip C: Boonyoung discusses his life as a monk; part 3 of 3
- 3.3 Film Worksheet: students assess their understanding of the case study film clips by linking ideas to the *Student Book*
- 3.3 Chant Audio Clip: a recording of the Buddhist chant, 'Om Mani Padme Hum'
- 3.3 Monastic Life Interactive Activity: students consider what life is like for a Buddhist monk
- 3.3 Lesson Player: a ready-to-go presentation with built-in resources and teacher notes
- 3 Image Gallery: a useful gallery of photos and illustrations from the chapter
- 3.3 Self-Assessment Sheet: students evaluate their learning against the lesson objectives

Ideas for starters

1. Use the starter in the *Student Book*.
2. Display the picture of the racing driver as students enter the room. Explain that it shows a particular child's ambition. Ask what they

think that child is doing now. Refer them to the picture caption and the photo of Boonyoung in the *Student Book*. Ask: do you think Boonyoung would still like to drive a racing car if he were given the chance?

3. Ask students how they think a Buddhist monk or nun in Britain spends their time from day to day. Revisit their responses at the end of the lesson.

Activity guidance

- Remind students to use what they learned in Unit 3.2 to help with Activity **1** in the *Student Book*.

- If you have time after Activity **2** in the *Student Book*, hot-seat Boonyoung – pick a student to play the monk – with each student asking their best one or two questions.

- For Activity **3** in the *Student Book*, you might like to explain the conventions of a diary entry, or show a couple of examples.

Ideas for plenaries

1. Use the Reflection from the *Student Book*. You could tell students what your own early ambitions were. Share ideas and explore some of the unexpected turns of events that can change the course of life.

2. Display and discuss students' posters from Activity **1** in the *Student Book*. Take a vote on which is the most successful.

3. Invite students to read out their diary entries for Activity **3** in the *Student Book*.

4. Conduct a short debate on whether or not students would want to become monks or nuns, and why or why not.

Further class and homework activities

1. Play a simple Buddhist chant (e.g. 3.3 Chant Audio Clip), asking students to listen carefully and try to make out words. Then ask them to join in. After a few minutes, ask them what their thoughts were while they were chanting.

2. Ask students to research how other Buddhist monks and nuns in different parts of the world spend their time.

They should write two or three paragraphs, drawing out experiences that are different from Boonyoung's.

3. 3.3 Film Worksheet on the *Buddhism Kerboodle*.

4. 3.3 Monastic Life Interactive Activity on the *Buddhism Kerboodle*.

5. Further suggestions on page 62 of this book.

3.4 Uncluttering Your Mind

The unit in brief

This unit explores the methods and purpose of meditation in more detail. It looks at how and where one lay Buddhist meditates and shares the insights of another practising Buddhist on the effect of meditation on daily life. The school of Pure Land Buddhism is also introduced.

Key ideas

- Meditation is often thought of as being essential to Buddhism
- Buddhists meditate to try to get away from surrounding distractions and simply be fully focused and aware, in order to find calm and clarity of thought
- Pure Land Buddhists believe that by meditating on Amida Buddha, they can be reborn into a 'Pure Land' and work towards Enlightenment

Useful Words

mandala, Pure Land, stupa

Skills practised

- Evaluation: considering the benefits of being able to rise above problems
- Analysis: considering which activities help to focus the mind
- Application: experiencing meditation and noting thoughts and feelings
- Interpretation: explaining how Buddhists use meditation
- Reflection: considering how important thoughts are

Resources

- 3.4 Meditation Film Clip: the Aldam family discusses how and why they meditate
- 3.4 Film Worksheet: students assess their understanding of the case study film clips by linking ideas to the *Student Book*
- 3.4 Led Meditation Audio Clip: a guided meditation for you to use with your students
- 3.4 Clarity Interactive Activity: students match up beginnings and endings to complete sentences about the key concepts from the unit
- 3.4 Lesson Player: a ready-to-go presentation with built-in resources and teacher notes
- 3 Image Gallery: a useful gallery of photos and illustrations from the chapter
- 3.4 Self-Assessment Sheet: students evaluate their learning against the lesson objectives

Ideas for starters

1. Display the picture of the person meditating as students enter the room. Ask them what the person is doing.

2. Ask if any students have ever meditated. If they are reluctant to share their experiences, simply ask if they would recommend the practice.

3. Use the second starter in the *Student Book*. What does 'rising above' the world and its problems mean to them? What benefits would that bring?

4. Ask students to write three questions they would like to ask about meditation on sticky notes. Collect these and try to answer them as a class at the end of the lesson.

Activity guidance

- As an alternative to Activity **2** in the *Student Book*, play 3.4 Led Meditation Audio Clip. Use sensitivity and clear guidance to ensure a comfortable and non-threatening environment. Students should write and share notes on their thoughts and feelings as in the original activity.

Ideas for plenaries

1. Use the Reflection from the *Student Book*. Extend this by asking the students if they agree with the Buddha when he said, 'all that we are is the result of what we have thought: it is founded on our thoughts, it is made up of our thoughts' (Dhammapada 1:1–2).

2. Encourage students to talk about their experience of meditation in Activity **2** in the *Student Book*. Did they enjoy it? Did they find it easy or difficult to focus?

3. Ask students for their views on the quotation from *Taming the Tiger Within* in the *Student Book*. Do they agree? Why might it be important to live in the moment? What could they do to try to live more in the moment?

4. Ask students to explain why meditation is the most important part of Buddhist worship.

Further class and homework activities

1. 3.4 Film Worksheet on the *Buddhism Kerboodle*.

2. 3.4 Clarity Interactive Activity on the *Buddhism Kerboodle*.

3. Further suggestions on page 62 of this book.

3.5 The Sound of One Hand Clapping

The unit in brief

This unit looks at Zen Buddhism. It explores the meaning of 'zen', the importance of meditation and the idea of living in the moment. It also gives students the opportunity to consider different methods of calming the mind.

Key ideas

- Zen Buddhists believe that Enlightenment is within everyone and that meditating to calm the mind is a way to achieve it
- Zen Buddhism advocates living in the moment
- Zen Buddhists often mediate on koans – riddles set by Zen masters

Useful Words

koan, zazen, Zen Buddhism

Skills practised

- Interpretation: explaining how Zen Buddhists use meditation, koans and gardens to calm the mind
- Analysis: comparing the practices of Zen and other Buddhists
- Enquiry: researching koans
- Reflection: considering what it means to live in the moment

Resources

- 3.5 Zen Worksheet: students consider how easy it is to live 'in the moment'
- 3.5 Belief and Practice Interactive Activity: students identify statements that reflect some of the beliefs and practices of Zen Buddhists
- 3.5 Lesson Player: a ready-to-go presentation with built-in resources and teacher notes
- 3 Image Gallery: a useful gallery of photos and illustrations from the chapter
- 3.5 Self-Assessment Sheet: students evaluate their learning against the lesson objectives

Ideas for starters

1. Ask students what they think of when they hear the term 'zen'. Do they know it from books or films? Explain that 'zen' comes from the Sanskrit word for 'meditation' or 'concentration'. Ask if they can guess how this links with Buddhism from what they know already.

2. Ask: what are people doing when they meditate? Write responses on the board and then refine the ideas at the end of the lesson.

3. Use the starter in the *Student Book*. Write responses on the board and revisit them at the end of the lesson. Given what they have learned about koans, what do they think now?

Activity guidance

- Before students tackle Activity **1** in the *Student Book*, look at the picture of the Zen garden together. What features do they notice? What do they think of the idea in the caption that change only comes from the person viewing the garden?

- Students may need the opportunity to do some more research to compile the table for Activity **2** in the *Student Book*.

- It might be a good idea to research some koans in preparation for Activity **3** in the *Student Book*. On this occasion, Wikipedia may not be a bad place to start; the entry for koans lists a few classic examples and references well-known collections.

Ideas for plenaries

1. Use the Reflection from the *Student Book*. You could give students the opportunity to find out how easy living in the moment is. Ask them to identify an object in the room that interests them and spend two minutes looking at it from their desk, trying to note every aspect of it. Then ask them how many times they had to keep pulling their mind back to the object.

2. Based on the table they made for Activity **2** in the *Student Book*, ask students to write a paragraph explaining some of the diversity in Buddhist belief and practice.

3. Ask students to share some of the koans they found for Activity **3** in the *Student Book*. Discuss which they find the most thought-provoking.

4. How might the Zen practice of meditating with eyes open be a different experience to that of meditating with eyes closed?

Further class and homework activities

1. 'Zen is the purest form of Buddhism.' Ask students to use what they have learned so far to write a response to the statement.

2. Ask students to make notes on, or draw a picture to represent, how they think their life would be different if they focused on living in the moment more.

3. You could use 3.5 Zen Worksheet on the *Buddhism Kerboodle* to support the Reflection in the *Student Book*.

4. 3.5 Belief and Practice Interactive Activity on the *Buddhism Kerboodle*.

5. Further suggestions on page 62 of this book.

6. Ask students to design a Zen garden, taking Zen practices into account.

3.6 The Happiest Man in the World?

The unit in brief

This unit looks at the life and work of Buddhist monk Matthieu Ricard, who has been scientifically 'proven' to be the happiest man in the world. It also explores ideas on what does and does not make people happy.

Key ideas

- There seem to be scientific links between meditation and health and happiness
- Ricard believes that happiness can be taught and learned, and that the Buddhist way of life increases happiness
- He believes money does not buy happiness but can be used to make people in need happier

Useful Words

PhD

Skills practised

- Analysis: exploring the link between meditation and happiness
- Enquiry: researching a famous Buddhist and his quotations
- Literacy: writing a biography entry and a letter
- Teamwork: planning and performing a play on how money can make people more or less happy
- Interpretation: explaining how following the Middle Way can bring happiness
- Reflection: considering the nature of happiness

Resources

- 3.6 Poster Worksheet: students design a poster to promote happiness within the school environment
- 3.6 World's Happiest Man? Interactive Activity: students select statements that relate to the life and beliefs of Matthieu Ricard
- 3.6 Lesson Player: a ready-to-go presentation with built-in resources and teacher notes
- 3 Image Gallery: a useful gallery of photos and illustrations from the chapter
- 3.6 Self-Assessment Sheet: students evaluate their learning against the lesson objectives

Ideas for starters

1. Use the first starter in the *Student Book*. Ask students to list the five things in life that bring them most happiness. Do not pass comment on their ideas, but at the end of the lesson ask if they want to change anything on their list.

2. Use the second starter in the *Student Book*. Ask: if happiness can be learned, how do we learn it? Give students five minutes to write a response and then encourage them to share some of their ideas.

3. Prepare a set of statements before the lesson along the lines of: 'I am happiest when...'. In class, indicate an invisible line across the room with 'agree' at one end and 'disagree' at the other. Read out each statement, giving students time to stand along the line to show whether they agree or disagree. Discuss results, drawing out the subjective nature of happiness.

Activity guidance

- Students can find information about Matthieu Ricard for Activity **1** in the *Student Book* on his personal website.

- Allow time for students to plan their play for Activity **2** in the *Student Book*. If they plan in detail, they may be able to improvise the dialogue in order to perform the play in the same lesson. Alternatively, you could allow more time for writing and practising the dialogue before the performance in a later lesson.

- Recap the Middle Way before students start Activity **3** in the *Student Book*.

Ideas for plenaries

1. Use the Reflection from the *Student Book* to start a class debate.

2. Ask students what they have learned about happiness in this lesson.

3. Ask students to work in pairs to explain the link between meditation and happiness in one sentence. Share and discuss.

4. Share some of the letters students wrote for Activity **3** in the *Student Book*.

Further class and homework activities

1. Discuss whether the happiness of some people means the unhappiness of others. Identify examples when this might be the case.

2. Ask students to make a collage of pictures of the things that make them happy.

3. 3.6 Poster Worksheet on the *Buddhism Kerboodle* would make a good homework task.

4. 3.6 World's Happiest Man? Interactive Activity on the *Buddhism Kerboodle*.

5. Further suggestions on page 62 of this book.

Chapter 3 Further Suggestions

These suggestions are addressed directly to students.

3.1 What does it Mean to Belong?

1 Write a story from the perspective of a Buddhist monk or nun about life as an ordained Buddhist in a monastery. **

2 Find out about different kinds of religious communities around the world. They can be Buddhist communities or from other faiths you have studied. *

3 Think about the relationship between lay and ordained Buddhists and decide who you think gets the most practical benefit and who gets the most spiritual benefit from this relationship. ***

4 In small groups, choose one form of Buddhism that interests you and plan a presentation about it to give to the class. **

3.2 Same Faith, Different Ways

1 Find out about the festivals and celebrations of different Buddhist traditions. Make a leaflet that presents these clearly and in an interesting way. **

2 'Variety in Buddhist belief makes the study of Buddhism difficult.' Write a response to this statement. **

3 Find out about Pure Land Buddhism. Focus on where it is common, what the key beliefs and practices are and who follows it. ***

3.3 Special Feature: Let's Meet a Monk

1 Does monastery life appeal to you? Explain why or why not. *

2 Imagine you are Boonyoung. Write a series of social networking posts (of no more than 140 characters each) that describe a typical day, including how you feel about it. **

3 'The Sangha is the most important of the Three Jewels.' Write a response to this statement. ***

3.4 Uncluttering Your Mind

1 Meditation is not just for Buddhists. Find out about meditation in other religions you have studied. *

2 Do you think images can help to focus the mind? Find out what images people use for meditation and how they are helpful. *

3 'Meditation is at the heart of Buddhist practice.' Explain your response to this statement. **

3.5 The Sound of One Hand Clapping

1 Make a poster explaining the basics of Zen Buddhism. *

2 Find out about Zen gardens. From your research, explain why they are designed in the way that they are. **

3 Think of some koans of your own. Be prepared to explain why they might be effective. ***

4 Research other ways that Zen Buddhists express their faith. *

5 'There is more than one way to reach Enlightenment.' Write a response to this statement, with reference to the different traditions of Buddhism you have learned about. ***

3.6 The Happiest Man in the World?

1 With his academic talents, Matthieu Ricard could probably have done many other jobs. Do you think he made a good choice when he decided to become a Buddhist monk? Explain your answer. ***

2 'Happiness is a skill. It requires effort and time.' Do you agree with this statement? How much time do you spend working on your happiness? **

Chapter 3 Assessment

Assessment in the *Student Book*

You will find an assessment task at the end of every chapter that focuses on AT2. In this chapter, the task asks students to answer two questions about commitments and lifestyles of Buddhist monks and nuns, in a format of their choice.

In the *Student Book* (and on the supporting worksheets), you'll find guidance about levels of assessment that you can use to help your students understand what their work should include. You could ask them to use these criteria for self- or peer-assessment once they've completed the task.

Assessment Task for Chapter 3 (pages **50–51** of the *Buddhism Student Book*)

Objectives

- Explain the commitments and lifestyle of Buddhist monks and nuns
- Reflect on and evaluate your own character and ideas about life
- Compare your views with the Buddhist lifestyles you have studied

Task

Draw on your learning about the commitments and lifestyle of Buddhist monks and nuns to answer these questions.

1. What is life like for a Buddhist monk or nun? Describe and explain the commitments made by bhikkhus. You can explore this within any strand of Buddhism.
2. Could you imagine ever being a Buddhist monk or nun? Reflect on your own character and beliefs to answer the question carefully.

You can choose how to present your responses. For example, you could write an essay, a letter to a friend, a series of diary entries or make a presentation.

Assessment in *Kerboodle*

On the *Buddhism Kerboodle*, you'll find resources to use when introducing the assessment task to the class.

You can use the *Chapter 3 Assessment Task Presentation* as a front-of-class tool to help your students unpack the assessment criteria, and understand what is expected of them.

Chapter 3 Assessment Worksheets accompany the task, so that once you finish the presentation, your students can easily get started.

Auto-marked tests

The *Buddhism Kerboodle* also contains auto-marked tests for each chapter to help save you time setting questions and marking for AT1. The test for this chapter contains 15 questions and will take most students about half an hour. Test results are automatically stored in the markbook.

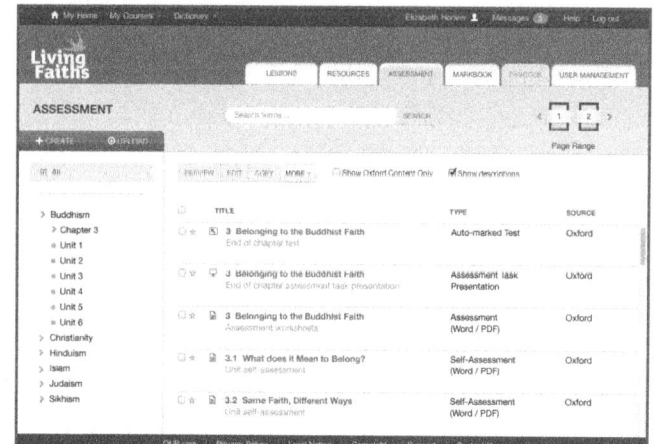

▲ Assessment resources for Chapter 3 on the *Buddhism Kerboodle*

Digital markbook

A markbook and a reporting function complete the *Kerboodle* assessment package, so you can keep all your students' test results and assessment scores in one place. This can include the auto-marked tests as well as pieces of work you or the students have marked by hand.

Chapter 4 Overview
Raising Questions, Exploring Answers

Helping you deliver KS3 RE

This chapter addresses these areas of the Programme of Study:

Key concepts

Values and commitments
- Understand how moral values and a sense of obligation can come from beliefs and experience
- Evaluate their own and others' values in order to make informed, rational and imaginative choices

Key processes

Learning about religion
- Evaluate how religious beliefs and teachings inform answers to ultimate questions and ethical issues

Learning from religion
- Reflect on the relationship between beliefs, teachings, world issues and ultimate questions

The big picture

These are the key ideas behind this chapter:

- The happiness and spiritual development of a country is just as important as its material development.
- Following a policy of non-violence in difficult circumstances is not easy.
- The current Dalai Lama is well known for his wisdom.
- Consumerism and being able to have whatever one wants are not necessarily good things.
- Buddhism teaches that craving causes suffering and it can never be satisfied.
- Buddhists believe that reason and experience are important, and that Buddhist principles are compatible with science.

Chapter outline

Use this to give students a mental roadmap for the chapter:

4.1 Gross National Happiness – introduces this concept and explores how it impacts on Bhutan and how it might impact on Britain

4.2 Faith Under Pressure – looks at the impact of Chinese occupation in Tibet and examines the effectiveness of peaceful protest in potentially violent circumstances, using Burma as another example

4.3 The Wisdom of Tenzin Gyatso, the Dalai Lama – explores the life, work, words and actions of the current Dalai Lama and considers what makes someone wise; includes a case study

4.4 The Challenges of Consumerism – examines the effects of consumerism on society and individuals, including through case studies

4.5 Is Buddhism Compatible with Science? – explores the relationship between science and faith with particular focus on Buddhism and modern Britain

Opportunities for assessment

Summative assessments on the *Buddhism Kerboodle* include auto-marked tests, interactive activities and self-assessment worksheets.

The end-of-chapter assessment task in the *Student Book* provides formative assessment. Supporting materials for the assessment task can be found on the *Buddhism Kerboodle*, such as the Assessment Task Presentation and related worksheets.

There are other opportunities for assessment too. For example, you could use some of the activities or reflection points throughout each *Student Book* unit, or some of the 'Further suggestions' at the end of this chapter.

Getting ready for this chapter

- Familiarize yourself with some of the teachings of the current Dalai Lama so that you can encourage in-depth discussion, especially in Unit 4.3.
- In preparation for Unit 4.1, you could pull out some key results of the UK's first National Wellbeing Project – they appear on the website of the Office for National Statistics. You might also wish to find recent or current news stories about Bhutan's policies to promote Gross National Happiness.
- Locate a large map of Tibet and the surrounding countries, or display the map in the *Student Book*, for Unit 4.2. You could do some background research on the peaceful uprising of Tibetan people in 1959 in protest against Chinese occupation.

Objectives and outcomes for this chapter

Objectives	Unit	Outcomes
Most students will:		Most students will be able to:
• identify why the King of Bhutan took his people's happiness so seriously • identify what features determine Gross National Happiness • reflect on what Gross National Happiness might mean in Britain today.	**4.1**	• explain how the King of Bhutan's faith impacted on his ideas about government • discuss features determining Gross National Happiness within the context of Britain • say whether they think happiness depends on more than having more money or possessions.
• explain why some Buddhists get involved in political conflicts • examine whether political activity is in line with Buddhist teaching • reflect on their own attitudes to challenging injustice.	**4.2**	• describe how Tibetans responded to the conflict arising from Chinese occupation. • describe the peaceful political campaign of Aung San Suu Kyi • empathize with those in exile or detention.
• explore the life and philosophy of Tenzin Gyatso • examine the impact of his teachings on people's lives • reflect on and evaluate his wisdom.	**4.3**	• recount Tenzin Gyatso's history and explain what he has done and experienced • interpret one or more of his teachings in a modern context • explain the personal importance of the wisdom of people they respect.
• explain Buddhist teaching on craving • explore if it is possible for the modern world to learn from those teachings • reflect on their own attitude to wanting and having things.	**4.4**	• recount a personal story about the disappointment associated with craving • write about modern consumerism from a Buddhist point of view • say how much they are influenced by the impulse to have what they want.
• examine Buddhist responses to the scientific view of the world • ask questions about the relationship between science and faith • reflect on their own views about faith and science.	**4.5**	• describe ways in which Buddhists engage with modern science • write about the relationship between science and Buddhism • say whether they think faith and science can work together effectively.

The unit in brief

This unit introduces students to the Buddhist Kingdom of Bhutan and the king's ideas about the happiness of his people. It looks at the implementation of Gross National Happiness in Bhutan and how modern life has affected this ancient kingdom.

Key ideas

- Bhutan is well known for the concept of Gross National Happiness
- People's happiness cannot be measured purely by how much money their country makes – spiritual development is just as important as material development
- The behaviour seen on television can have a bad effect on the behaviour of ordinary people

Useful Words

GDP (Gross Domestic Product), GNH (Gross National Happiness)

Skills practised

- Interpretation: explaining why the King of Bhutan thought his people's happiness was so important
- Evaluation: considering the balance between spiritual and material happiness
- Enquiry: identifying the features that determine Gross National Happiness
- Analysis: discussing the link between what people watch and what they do
- Reflection: considering whether Gross National Happiness or Gross Domestic Product is more important

Resources

- 4.1 Island Worksheet: students design their own island based on the concept of Gross National Happiness
- 4.1 Gross National Happiness Interactive Activity: students complete paragraphs about the concept of Gross National Happiness introduced in the Buddhist kingdom of Bhutan
- 4.1 Lesson Player: a ready-to-go presentation with built-in resources and teacher notes
- 4 Image Gallery: a useful gallery of photos and illustrations from the chapter
- 4.1 Self-Assessment Sheet: students evaluate their learning against the lesson objectives

Ideas for starters

1. Discuss the starter in the *Student Book*. Draw out any links between the two concepts.

2. Ask students to imagine what a really happy society would be like and what its key characteristics would be. What do they think the benefits of a happier nation are?

3. Ask students to list five things that would make a whole country happy.

Activity guidance

• For Activity **1** in the *Student Book*, you could ask students to pretend they are the King of Bhutan and write a speech to his people, explaining his views.

• After students have listed their points for Activity **2a** in the *Student Book*, you could ask them to do some research on, or give them some key points from, the results of the UK's National Wellbeing Project. The key results appear on the website of the Office for National Statistics.

• You could introduce Activity **2b** in the *Student Book* with a couple of quotations: former US senator Robert Kennedy said that GDP 'measures everything [...] except that which makes life worthwhile'; on launching the UK National Wellbeing Project, David Cameron said, 'the country would be better off if we thought about wellbeing and quality of life as well as economic growth' and that 'this information [from the survey] will help government work out, with evidence, the best ways of trying to help to improve people's wellbeing'.

Ideas for plenaries

1. Use the Reflection from the *Student Book* to start discussion.

2. Ask students to present the speeches they wrote for Activity **2** in the *Student Book*.

3. As a class, look at the television schedule for the day. Do students think any particular programmes will have a good or bad effect on people?

4. Ask students to look carefully at the four principles for GNH and, for each one, list what examples they can think of to show how Britain puts these into practice. Do they think we could do more? If so, what?

Further class and homework activities

1. You could use 4.1 Island Worksheet on the *Buddhism Kerboodle* as a homework activity. The task could be extended by asking students to plan a special 'GNH Awareness Day' celebration that will be hosted on their island.

2. Ask students, perhaps for homework, to look up the teachings of the Mettā Sutta.

How might following these teachings lead to greater happiness for everyone?

3. 4.1 Gross National Happiness Interactive Activity on the *Buddhism Kerboodle*.

4. Further suggestions on page 76 of this book.

4.2 Faith Under Pressure

The unit in brief

This unit gives a very brief history of Tibetan Buddhism and its leader, the Dalai Lama. It examines the effectiveness of peaceful protest in potentially violent circumstances, and particular attention is given to the political campaign and house arrest of Aung San Suu Kyi.

Key ideas

- Tibet is a Buddhist country and its most senior spiritual and political leader is the Dalai Lama
- The current Dalai Lama fled from Chinese occupation of Tibet and now lives in India
- The Dalai Lama is well known for his work for peace
- Aung San Suu Kyi, a Buddhist politician, protested against the Burmese military government
- Suu Kyi used non-violent protest while under house arrest and her message was spread worldwide

Useful Words

Dalai Lama, lama

Skills practised

- Literacy: writing an article about the Tibetan uprising and a speech as the Dalai Lama
- Communication: writing a letter to Aung San Suu Kyi when she was under house arrest
- Evaluation: examining the role of the Dalai Lama
- Reflection: considering how Buddhists respond to conflict and what in life is worth defending
- Empathy: reflecting on how it might feel to be an exile

Resources

- 4.2 Suu Kyi Audio Clip: a first-person account of Buddhism in Burma and Aung San Suu Kyi
- 4.2 Newspaper Worksheet: students write a newspaper report on Aung San Suu Kyi's peaceful protest
- 4.2 Conflict Interactive Activity: students show their knowledge about two predominantly Buddhist countries
- 4.2 Lesson Player: a ready-to-go presentation with built-in resources and teacher notes
- 4 Image Gallery: a useful gallery of photos and illustrations from the chapter
- 4.2 Self-Assessment Sheet: students evaluate their learning against the lesson objectives

Ideas for starters

1. Using the first starter in the *Student Book*, encourage students to contribute to a mind-map on the board. Students could go on to make their own list of things they think are worth defending, justifying each choice with at least two reasons.

2. Ask students to discuss the second starter in the *Student Book* in pairs. Invite students to share their experiences with the class.

3. Display the map from Unit 4.1 and briefly discuss Tibet and Burma's significance and place in the world.

Activity guidance

•   Allow time for students to do some research to fill out the facts for Activity **2** in the *Student Book*. Students could use 4.2 Newspaper Worksheet to help them complete this activity – it includes a newspaper front page template. As an alternative to writing an article, students could present their findings as a news report for television.

•   To compare attitudes of other faiths to war and peace, see Unit 4.3 in the *Islam Student Book*, or Unit 5.5 in the *Judaism Student Book*.

Ideas for plenaries

1. Use the Reflection from the *Student Book* to spark discussion.

2. Nominate students to perform the speech they wrote for Activity **3** in the *Student Book*.

3. Ask students to write a text message explaining one thing they have learned about the people of Tibet or Burma.

4. 'The world needs spiritual leaders to guide how we live.' Organize a class debate presenting arguments for and against this statement.

Further class and homework activities

1. Ask students to write a short story about how they would feel if they lived in Tibet during occupation by the Chinese.

2. 4.2 Newspaper Worksheet on the *Buddhism Kerboodle* can be used as a way of completing Activity **2** in the *Student Book*.

3. 4.2 Conflict Interactive Activity on the *Buddhism Kerboodle*.

4. Further suggestions on page 76 of this book.

4.3 The Wisdom of Tenzin Gyatso, the Dalai Lama

The unit in brief

This unit explores the life, work, words and actions of the current Dalai Lama. It gives students the opportunity to consider what makes someone wise and to understand the importance of the Dalai Lama to a practising Buddhist.

Key ideas

- The current Dalai Lama is known for his wisdom, which often challenges the way people live
- His outlook and wisdom come from personal experience and his views are valued by world leaders
- The Dalai Lama's teachings appeal to a lot of people

Skills practised

- Enquiry: researching the life and work of the current Dalai Lama
- Interpretation: presenting the meaning of one of the Dalai Lama's teachings
- Evaluation: considering the impact of the Dalai Lama's teachings on people's lives
- Literacy: writing a speech to welcome the Dalai Lama
- Reflection: considering what makes someone wise and what reminds them of something or someone important

Resources

- 4.3 Blessing Strings Film Clip: Molly and her grandmother discuss when they heard the Dalai Lama teach in Manchester
- 4.3 Film Worksheet: students assess their understanding of the case study film clips by linking ideas to the *Student Book*
- 4.3 Quotations Audio Clip: a reading of the teachings of the Dalai Lama featured in this unit
- 4.3 Dalai Lama Interactive Activity: students select words to complete text about the teachings and philosophy of the Dalai Lama
- 4.3 Lesson Player: a ready-to-go presentation with built-in resources and teacher notes
- 4 Image Gallery: a useful gallery of photos and illustrations from the chapter
- 4.3 Self-Assessment Sheet: students evaluate their learning against the lesson objectives

Ideas for starters

1. Draw a stick person on the board and ask what a wise person looks like. Add to the drawing. Then ask how you can tell

someone is wise without looking at them. Encourage students to consider the inner characteristics and traits of the wise.

2. Use the starters in the *Student Book*. Students must be able to explain their reasons.

3. Ask students to choose another student they consider to be wise. Ask them to say what makes that person wise.

Activity guidance

- If students need inspiration for Activity **2** in the *Student Book*, encourage them to think of people who have fought for rights and freedom (e.g. Aung San Suu Kyi, Nelson Mandela, Emmeline Pankhurst, Martin Luther King) or who have made discoveries through feats of endurance (e.g. Sir Edmund Hillary, Robert Falcon Scott, Amelia Earhart, Christopher Columbus).

Ideas for plenaries

1. Use the Reflection from the *Student Book*.

2. Display the posters from Activity **1** in the *Student Book*. Ask students to comment on the quotations chosen and why they are so inspiring.

3. Display the case studies from Activity **2** in the *Student Book* and allow students to read one or two of them. Discuss and try to agree on what makes these people inspiring.

4. Ask some students to read the speeches they prepared for Activity **3** in the *Student Book*.

5. 'Happiness is not something ready made. It comes from your own actions.' Do students agree and for what reasons? Ask them how someone who believes this statement would live their life.

Further class and homework activities

1. Ask students to write a story or a poem about something that they wear or keep to remind themselves of something or someone that is important to them. They could also illustrate their work.

2. You could use 4.3 Film Worksheet on the *Buddhism Kerboodle* after watching the film clip but before attempting the further activity suggested above. This will encourage students to think about any items that remind them of an important person in their lives.

3. 4.3 Dalai Lama Interactive Activity on the *Buddhism Kerboodle*.

4. Further suggestions on page 76 of this book.

4.4 The Challenges of Consumerism

The unit in brief

This unit examines the effects of consumerism on society and individuals. It evaluates Buddhist teaching on craving in light of the modern consumerist world. It also gives students the opportunity to consider their own relationship with the desire to acquire things.

Key ideas

- Consumerism and being able to have whatever one wants are not necessarily good things
- Buddhism teaches that craving causes suffering and can never be satisfied
- Many people think that a society driven purely by consumerism is unsustainable

Skills practised

- Reflection: considering the implications of living in a consumerist society
- Literacy: writing an article for a fashion magazine and a story about the disappointment associated with craving
- Interpretation: explaining the Buddhist perspective on consumerism
- Evaluation: debating whether consumerism is a good or a bad thing

Resources

- 4.4 Possessions Film Clip A: Molly considers the implications of a consumerist society
- 4.4 Possessions Film Clip B: Tom explains how Buddhism helps him deal with craving
- 4.4 Film Worksheet: students assess their understanding of the case study film clips by linking ideas to the *Student Book*
- 4.4 Craving Interactive Activity: students select statements that reflect Buddhist views on wanting and having material possessions
- 4.4 Lesson Player: a ready-to-go presentation with built-in resources and teacher notes
- 4 Image Gallery: a useful gallery of photos and illustrations from the chapter
- 4.4 Self-Assessment Sheet: students evaluate their learning against the lesson objectives

Ideas for starters

1. Use the starters in the *Student Book* to stimulate discussion. You could revisit the second question at the end of the lesson.

2. Ask students to list some of the branded goods they own. Ask them why they have chosen those brands and why they like them.

3. Look at the picture of the shop in the *Student Book* and ask the question in the caption. Ask students how they felt about the thing they were desperate to buy a few months after they had actually bought it.

Activity guidance

- As an alternative to writing a story for Activity **2** in the *Student Book*, students could create a cartoon on the same theme.

- You could prepare for the class debate in Activity **3** in the *Student Book* by listing ideas for and against on the board. Students could consider the effects of producing goods on the environment and on workers in poor countries as well as the effects of greed on consumers. Then let them prepare their own arguments. Take a vote at the end of the debate and ask a few students, for and against, to state one reason each for their vote.

Ideas for plenaries

1. Ask students to respond to the Reflection in the *Student Book* by writing a short personal statement. Then ask whether they think the impulse is positive or negative.

2. Ask students to read out the stories they produced for Activity **2** in the *Student Book*.

3. Ask students to write a text message or short email to a friend explaining one thing they learned in this lesson. They could start with, 'Did you know that…?'.

Further class and homework activities

1. For homework, ask students to research how Freecycle works. How are such movements challenging our consumer-focused lifestyle?

2. Students could create a slogan and design for an anti-consumerist t-shirt to be sold in aid of a charity.

3. 4.4 Film Worksheet on the *Buddhism Kerboodle*.

4. 4.4 Craving Interactive Activity on the *Buddhism Kerboodle*.

5. Further suggestions on page 76 of this book.

4.5 Is Buddhism Compatible with Science?

The unit in brief

This unit explores the relationship between science and faith with a particular focus on how Buddhism and modern science can work together. It also explores the balance between faith and science in modern Britain.

Key ideas

- It has become popular to say that science and faith are not compatible
- Buddhism has responded positively to modern technology and science and the Dalai Lama is keen to improve this relationship
- It is thought that Buddhism can help develop a clearer understanding of the workings of the mind
- Buddhists believe that reason and experience are important, and that the Buddhist faith is compatible with science

Useful Words

neuroscience

Skills practised

- Interpretation: explaining Buddhist responses to the scientific view of the world
- Reflection: expressing their own views on the relationship between science and faith
- Literacy: writing a summary and writing a letter
- Teamwork: discussing points and recording the outcome

Resources

- 📄 4.5 Poster Worksheet: students design a poster that shows how Buddhism and science can contribute to each other
- 🖱 4.5 Science Interactive Activity: students read statements about the relationship between Buddhism and science and decide which ones are true
- 🎓 4.5 Lesson Player: a ready-to-go presentation with built-in resources and teacher notes
- 🖥 4 Image Gallery: a useful gallery of photos and illustrations from the chapter
- 📄 4.5 Self-Assessment Sheet: students evaluate their learning against the lesson objectives

Ideas for starters

1. Use the starters in the *Student Book*.
2. Write 'Science' and 'Faith' at opposite ends of the board. Ask students if there are any ways of making linking lines between the two.

3. Write the two words as above and ask students to stand by whichever they put most trust in. They must be prepared to explain their choice.

4. Give students two minutes to write a response to the statement: 'Faith and science are incompatible.'

Activity guidance

- After students have compiled their bullet points for Activity **2** in the *Student Book*, ask pairs to join in groups of four to discuss and agree on their five best points, which they should then be invited to share with the class.

- Remind students to structure their letters for Activity **4** in the *Student Book* in order to produce a clear argument. Encourage them to write a short paragraph introducing the topic, followed by two or three paragraphs setting out the main points of their argument, and then a final paragraph explaining their conclusion.

Ideas for plenaries

1. Use the Reflection from the *Student Book* to start discussion.

2. Use the question, 'Does knowing more about science take away the mystery and wonder of the world, or add to it?' to start discussion.

3. Choose students to read the letter they wrote for Activity **4** in the *Student Book*.

4. Ask students to revisit their responses to the statement: 'Faith and science are incompatible.' Ask if they have changed their views and to explain why.

Further class and homework activities

1. Ask students to write a summary comparing the relationship between Buddhism and science with the relationship other faiths they have studied have with science. For more information, see Unit 4.1 in the *Christianity Student Book*, or Unit 4.3 in the *Sikhism Student Book*.

2. You could use 4.5 Poster Worksheet on the *Buddhism Kerboodle* at the end of the lesson or set it as a homework task.

3. 4.5 Science Interactive Activity on the *Buddhism Kerboodle*.

4. Further suggestions on page 76 of this book.

Chapter 4 Further Suggestions

These suggestions are addressed directly to students.

4.1 Gross National Happiness

1 Start a scrapbook or a collage of things that make you happy. Write captions to explain why you have included each picture. *

2 Find out how the policy of Gross National Happiness affects life in Bhutan. **

3 Make an advertisement or brochure to persuade people to visit Bhutan. **

4 Prepare arguments, either for or against, for a debate about the statement: 'Violence on TV is a bad influence on attitudes and behaviour and should be banned.' ***

4.2 Faith Under Pressure

1 Research the history and culture of Tibet. Make a presentation about Tibet that compares the past and present, focusing on the status of Buddhism. ***

2 Choose one of the previous Dalai Lamas. You could do some research, starting by searching the Encyclopaedia Britannica's website. Create a poster that shows who your chosen Dalai Lama was, what he did and how he led Tibetan Buddhists. **

3 Compare Buddhist teachings about non-violence with the teachings of other faiths you have studied. Do the actual practices of some followers differ from the teachings? ***

4.3 The Wisdom of Tenzin Gyatso, the Dalai Lama

1 Make a collage of pictures of people who you think are wise. Then add quotations from each person that demonstrate their wisdom. *

2 Prepare a presentation to your class about the life and work of Tenzin Gyatso. Focus on what you think are the most important things he has done. **

3 With other members of your class, interview other students and teachers about who they consider to be a wise person and why. If there are cameras available, and the interviewee agrees, you could even film the interviews. **

4 Write a definition of what wisdom is. Is it necessary to be religious to be wise? ***

4.4 The Challenges of Consumerism

1 'I shop, therefore I am.' Write a story or poem based on this quotation. **

2 Research which clothing companies based on the UK high street have ethical policies regarding the production of their clothes. Write a report on your findings. ***

3 What do the other faiths you have studied say about how people spend their money? Compare and contrast these teachings with Buddhist teachings. **

4.5 Is Buddhism Compatible with Science?

1 Create a poster showing the relationship between science and Buddhism. Make it as visually exciting as you can. *

2 Find out about scientists who are also religious believers. You could consider scientists such as Issac Newton, Albert Einstein, Charles Darwin, or Michael Faraday, and start by doing an Internet search. How do these scientists balance their faith and scientific work? **

3 From what you know about the relationship between science and Buddhism, explain how Buddhism can be viewed as a faith that works with science. ***

Chapter 4 Assessment

Assessment in the *Student Book*

You will find an assessment task at the end of every chapter that focuses on AT2. In this chapter, the task asks students to prepare a presentation on Buddhism's place in the modern world and in the future.

In the *Student Book* (and on the supporting worksheets), you'll find guidance about levels of assessment that you can use to help your students understand what their work should include. You could ask them to use these criteria for self- or peer-assessment once they've completed the task.

<table>
<tr><td colspan="2">

Living Faiths Assessment

Student Book
- Assessment Task
- Levels Guidance

Kerboodle
- Auto-Marked Test
- Assessment Task Presentation
- Assessment Worksheets
</td></tr>
</table>

Assessment Task for Chapter 4 (pages **62–63** of the *Buddhism Student Book*)

Objectives

- Evaluate and explain the place of Buddhism in the modern world
- Reflect on the history and heritage of Buddhism
- Develop interesting ways of presenting your learning about Buddhism

Task

Prepare a presentation for an assembly on the theme 'Buddhism: religion of the future'. Use what you have learned about the development of Buddhism and how it is practised in the modern world. Explain what it can teach the modern world about the way we live now and how we might live in the future. Create some interesting visual resources to make your presentation more engaging.

Assessment in *Kerboodle*

On the *Buddhism Kerboodle*, you'll find resources to use when introducing the assessment task to the class.

You can use the *Chapter 4 Assessment Task Presentation* as a front-of-class tool to help your students unpack the assessment criteria, and understand what is expected of them.

Chapter 4 Assessment Worksheets accompany the task, so that once you finish the presentation, your students can easily get started.

Auto-marked tests

The *Buddhism Kerboodle* also contains auto-marked tests for each chapter to help save you time setting questions and marking for AT1. The test for this chapter contains 15 questions and will take most students about half an hour. Test results are automatically stored in the markbook.

Digital markbook

A markbook and a reporting function complete the *Kerboodle* assessment package, so you can keep all your students' test results and assessment scores in one place. This can include the auto-marked tests as well as pieces of work you or the students have marked by hand.

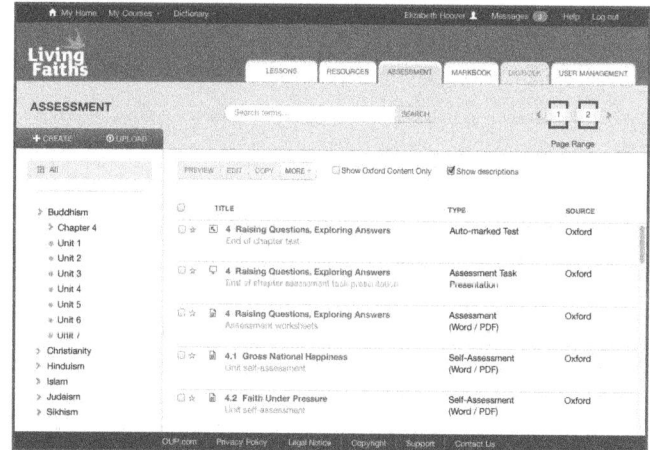

▲ Assessment resources for Chapter 4 on the *Buddhism Kerboodle*

Helping you deliver KS3 RE

This chapter addresses these areas of the Programme of Study:

Key concepts

Practices and ways of life
- Understand that religious practices are diverse, change over time and are influenced by culture

Identity, diversity and belonging
- Explore the variety, difference and relationships that exist within and between religions, values and beliefs

Key processes

Learning about religion
- Investigate the impact of religious beliefs and teachings on individuals, communities and societies, the reasons for commitment and the causes of diversity
- Analyse religious beliefs, arguments and ideas

Learning from religion
- Evaluate beliefs, commitments and the impact of religion in the contemporary world

The big picture

These are the key ideas behind this chapter:

- Some people find Buddhism attractive because it seems to complement modern life.
- Buddhist customs and ceremonies to mark rites of passage vary around the world.
- Equality between men and women is an important concept in Buddhism.
- Buddhists believe in the value of life and that how money is earned is important.
- Buddhists think that animal rights and non-violence are important.
- Prominent Buddhists can be a real force for peace.

Chapter outline

Use this to give students a mental roadmap for the chapter:

5.1 British Buddhists – Who Are They? – explores how Buddhism was introduced to Britain and what it means to be a British Buddhist, including through a case study

5.2 Growing Up: The Buddhist Way – focuses on the importance of equality, love and compassion in Buddhist relationships and how Buddhists mark rites of passage

5.3 How Much is Enough? – explores the value of money, material possessions and life, as well as Buddhist views on poverty and wealth

5.4 Special Feature: Do Animals have Rights? – looks at Buddhist views on animal rights and how Buddhists interpret their beliefs for life in the modern world; includes case studies

5.5 Can Non-Violence Really Work? – examines Buddhist beliefs on non-violence and how some actions are informed by those beliefs to a greater or lesser extent; includes a case study

5.6 Thich Nhat Hanh: Man of Peace – introduces the life and work of the Zen master Thich Nhat Hanh and explores what motivates people to help others

Opportunities for assessment

Summative assessments on the *Buddhism Kerboodle* include auto-marked tests, interactive activities and self-assessment worksheets.

The end-of-chapter assessment task in the *Student Book* provides formative assessment. Supporting materials for the assessment task can be found on the *Buddhism Kerboodle*, such as the Assessment Task Presentation and related worksheets.

There are other opportunities for assessment too. For example, you could use some of the activities or reflection points throughout each *Student Book* unit, or some of the 'Further suggestions' at the end of this chapter.

Getting ready for this chapter

- Make sure you are aware of any specific current issues that face Buddhists in Britain and the wider world. Collect newspaper articles on relevant issues.
- Collect pictures of the ways animals are used for a starter in Unit 5.4. For example: for work (guide dogs, police dogs, sheep dogs), for entertainment, or for medical or cosmetic testing.
- Find out about Thich Nhat Hanh so you can encourage in-depth discussion in Unit 5.6. His official website is a useful point of reference.

- If possible, invite members of the local Buddhist community to come into school and share how their faith affects their career choices, especially in preparation for Units 5.4 and 5.5.

Objectives and outcomes for this chapter

Objectives	Unit	Outcomes
Most students will:		Most students will be able to:
• examine the spread of Buddhism in Britain • evaluate the place of Buddhism in modern Britain • reflect on Britain as a multifaith society.	5.1	• recount the history of Buddhism in Britain • explain why Buddhism appeals to some modern Britons • evaluate the benefits of a multifaith society and of faiths uniting to solve the world's problems.
• identify how Buddhists approach important stages in life • analyse what it means to grow up as a Buddhist • reflect on the importance of equality.	5.2	• describe how Buddhists mark various rites of passage • explain how Buddhist children are brought up • discuss and communicate how important equality is.
• explain what Buddhism teaches about wealth and poverty • analyse some of the Buddha's teachings about money • reflect on what it means to be rich or poor.	5.3	• describe how Buddhists follow the Middle Way • interpret a Buddhist moral story on the motivation behind charitable giving • evaluate whether it is better to have virtue or material wealth.
• explain Buddhist views on animal rights • identify the significance of kamma in relation to this issue • reflect on how they think animals should be treated.	5.4	• interpret Buddhist views on doing no harm to any living creature • explain how taking good or bad actions creates good or bad kamma • analyse whether they think human life is more important than animal life and whether all animals can be treated with respect.
• develop further understanding of Buddhist teaching on conflict • explain different views on the use of violence and non-violence • reflect on the place of non-violence in the modern world.	5.5	• consolidate existing and new understanding of the Buddhist belief in non-violence • reconcile actions of Buddhists that seem violent with their belief in non-violence • analyse how a belief in non-violence can be followed by ordinary people in the modern world.
• investigate Thich Nhat Hanh's work in promoting peace • identify why Buddhists work for positive changes in the world • reflect on what motivates people to help others.	5.6	• describe Engaged Buddhism and the work of Thich Nhat Hanh in promoting peace • explain why Buddhists and other people engage in social action • analyse whether people need to have a faith to want to help others or not.

5.1 British Buddhists – Who Are They?

The unit in brief

This unit looks at the history and development of Buddhism in Britain. It gives students the opportunity to explore what life is like for Buddhists in Britain today. It also introduces the Dalai Lama's view that interfaith dialogue is important.

Key ideas

- Britain is a multicultural, multifaith society
- Buddhism came to Britain at the beginning of the twentieth century, with another rise of interest in the latter half of the century
- Buddhism is attractive to some people because it seems to complement modern life
- British Buddhists can worship at home, in a temple or attend retreats

Useful Words

multicultural, multifaith, retreat

Skills practised

- Reflection: considering their own preference for fitting in or standing out
- Evaluation: weighing up the positive and negative aspects of being a British Buddhist
- Analysis: considering what aspects of Buddhism appeal to British people
- Problem-solving: debating and concluding how religious leaders might unite to solve the world's problems
- Teamwork: planning events and celebrations for One World Week

Resources

- 5.1 British Buddhism Film Clip: Tom considers whether his faith affects how others treat him
- 5.1 Film Worksheet: students assess their understanding of the case study film clips by linking ideas to the *Student Book*
- 5.1 True or False Interactive Activity: students decide whether statements about Buddhism in Britain are true or false
- 5.1 Lesson Player: a ready-to-go presentation with built-in resources and teacher notes
- 5 Image Gallery: a useful gallery of photos and illustrations from the chapter
- 5.1 Self-Assessment Sheet: students evaluate their learning against the lesson objectives

Activity guidance

- The most useful ideas for the Reflection in the *Student Book* might come from a small group or a whole-class discussion. Students could then write two or three paragraphs independently to draw their own conclusions.

- Activity **2** in the *Student Book* refers to One World Week, the annual development charity event (not the University of Warwick student event) that takes place each autumn. Information can be found on the official website. You could also plan a series of events around Interfaith Week, which usually takes place in November.

- To compare how other faiths exist and coexist in modern Britain, see Unit 5.6 in the *Hinduism Student Book*, Unit 5.6 in the *Christianity Student Book*, or Unit 5.5 in the *Judaism Student Book*.

Ideas for plenaries

1. Use the Reflection from the *Student Book*.

2. Take feedback from Activity **1** in the *Student Book*.

3. Organize a short class debate on the topic: Faith is determined by geography.

4. To stretch students, challenge them by holding a class or group discussion on whether it is possible for someone to say they are Buddhist without being religious.

5.2 Growing Up: The Buddhist Way

The unit in brief

This unit focuses on relationships in Buddhism and the importance of equality, love and compassion. It looks at how Buddhists mark rites of passage and the place of women in Buddhism.

Key ideas

- There are no universal ceremonies in Buddhism to mark rites of passage
- In some countries, Buddhist children spend some time living as a monk or nun
- Equality between men and women is an important concept in Buddhism

Skills practised

- Reflection: considering their own views on and experiences of equality
- Thinking: identifying rites of passage from their own lives
- Interpretation: explaining why there are no universal rites of passage in Buddhism and how Buddhist teachings can guide family relationships
- Evaluating: considering the importance of equality
- Literacy: writing a play about inequality and a short guide to relationships
- Application: exploring the issues around inequality in a play

Resources

- 5.2 Questionnaire Worksheet: students interview family members and record their views on equality
- 5.2 Equality and Family Interactive Activity: students consider what it means to grow up as a Buddhist
- 5.2 Lesson Player: a ready-to-go presentation with built-in resources and teacher notes
- 5 Image Gallery: a useful gallery of photos and illustrations from the chapter
- 5.2 Self-assessment Sheet: students evaluate their learning against the lesson objectives

Ideas for starters

1. Use the first starter in the *Student Book* to start a class discussion about equality. Ask students to explain their thoughts, with clear justification for their answer. You could broaden this into a wider debate on whether society should treat everyone equally and how equality could be achieved.

2. Use the second starter in the *Student Book*. Ask students to write their ideas on separate sticky notes. Draw a line on the board with 'Birth' at one end and 'Death' at the other. Ask

students, in turn, to place their sticky notes where they belong on the line.

3. Look at the picture of the children in image **a** together. Ask students how they would feel if they had to live in a Buddhist monastery, without their family, for six months.

Activity guidance

- For Activity **2** in the *Student Book*, first start with a class discussion on the questions. Encourage students to make notes. Then organize students into groups of three or four. Give them time to decide on their storyline and allocate characters before they start to write a short play as a team.

Ideas for plenaries

1. Discuss the Reflection from the *Student Book*.

2. Watch the plays that students prepared for Activity **2** in the *Student Book*. Ask the audience to think about how well each play depicts inequality and offers a clear message. Ask for feedback on each play, perhaps in the form of two things that are good and one thing that could be improved.

3. Discuss the issues involved in trying to achieve equality in our society.

4. Ask students to write a paragraph explaining the importance of love and compassion in Buddhist relationships.

Further class and homework activities

1. Ask students to compare and contrast Buddhist teachings about equality and family with those of another faith they have studied. For more information see Unit 5.4 in the *Hinduism Student Book* or Chapter 5 in the *Islam Student Book*.

2. Students could use 5.2 Questionnaire Worksheet on the *Buddhism Kerboodle*, either in class or at home, to record friends' and family members' opinions on equality. This can then feed into their work on Activity **2** in the *Student Book*.

3. 5.2 Equality and Family Interactive Activity on the *Buddhism Kerboodle*.

4. Further suggestions on page 92 of this book.

5.3 How Much is Enough?

The unit in brief

This unit explores the value of money, material possessions and life. It explores Buddhist views on poverty, wealth, how to earn a living and charity.

Key ideas

- The Buddha taught that neither wealth nor poverty brings contentment
- He taught that seeing the value in life is important, not material possessions
- Buddhists do not think it is wrong to earn money, but that how they earn it is important
- Buddhists believe that using money to help others creates good kamma

Skills practised

- Analysis: considering what outward signs show that a person is rich
- Thinking: considering how much money is enough
- Communication: explaining on a poster whether the Middle Way is a good way to live
- Interpretation: explaining the Buddha's teachings on wealth and poverty
- Literacy: writing the script for a moral play
- Team work: producing and performing a moral play
- Reflection: considering whether virtue is more important than material wealth

Resources

- 5.3 Prince Payasi Audio Clip: a reading of the tale from the Payasi Sutta featured in the *Student Book*

- 5.3 Drama Worksheet: students storyboard a television drama of the story of Prince Payasi

- 5.3 Good Kamma Interactive Activity: students drag events in a story about the importance of giving into the correct order

- 5.3 Lesson Player: a ready-to-go presentation with built-in resources and teacher notes

- 5 Image Gallery: a useful gallery of photos and illustrations from the chapter

- 5.3 Self-assessment Sheet: students evaluate their learning against the lesson objectives

Ideas for starters

1. Use the first starter in the *Student Book* and then discuss the sketches.

2. Use the second starter in the *Student Book*. Ask students to write a three-sentence response to the question.

3. Ask students how much money they expect to earn when they are older and what they want to do with it.

Activity guidance

- You could organize Activity **4** in the *Student Book* as a whole-class play. Assign roles or allow students to allocate them: a narrator, Prince Payasi and Uttara. The rest will make up 'the people' and perhaps certain prominent individuals. You could arrange for the final performance to be for a school assembly, so allow students time to perfect their script and practise their acting.

- To help make interfaith links regarding wealth and charity, see Unit 3.2 in the *Islam Student Book* or Unit 5.4 in the *Judaism Student Book*.

Ideas for plenaries

1. Use the Reflection from the *Student Book*.

2. Revisit students' responses to the second starter in the *Student Book*. Have they changed their ideas now?

3. Display the posters from Activity **1** in the *Student Book* and ask individuals to explain theirs.

4. Display the emblems from Activity **2** in the *Student Book*. Students could vote on which one works best.

5. Ask students to write a paragraph summarizing what they have learned in this unit.

Further class and homework activities

1. Students could use 5.3 Drama Worksheet on the *Buddhism Kerboodle* as an alternative way of completing Activity **4** in the *Student Book*.

2. Ask students to make a list of all the ways Buddhist teachings affect choices about wealth and employment.

3. 5.3 Good Kamma Interactive Activity on the *Buddhism Kerboodle*.

4. Further suggestions on page 92 of this book.

5.4 Special Feature: Do Animals have Rights?

The unit in brief

This unit explores Buddhist beliefs and views on animal rights. It looks at how Buddhists practise these beliefs in real circumstances in the real world. It also gives students the opportunity to reflect on their own views on animal rights.

Key ideas

- Buddhists try not to cause harm to any living creature
- Many Buddhists choose to be vegetarians
- Most Buddhists think animal rights are important

Skills practised

- Interpretation: explaining why Buddhists respect all living creatures
- Empathy: considering whether animals have the same rights as humans
- Analysis: considering whether humans are responsible for animal care
- Evaluation: debating whether human life is more important than animal life
- Speaking: taking part in a debate on the importance of animal life
- Teamwork: preparing an assembly on animal rights
- Reflection: considering their own views on animal rights

Resources

- 5.4 Animals Film Clip A: Mrs Aldam talks about the importance of free range farming
- 5.4 Animals Film Clip B: Boonyoung gives his views on animal rights
- 5.4 Film Worksheet: students assess their understanding of the case study film clips by linking ideas to the *Student Book*
- 5.4 Animal Rights Interactive Activity: students complete a paragraph about Buddhist views on animal rights
- 5.4 Lesson Player: a ready-to-go presentation with built-in resources and teacher notes
- 5 Image Gallery: a useful gallery of photos and illustrations from the chapter
- 5.4 Self-assessment Sheet: students evaluate their learning against the lesson objectives

Ideas for starters

1. Display the picture of the lamb as students enter the room. Ask how the picture makes them feel. Then ask them how they feel about the lamb being used as food for humans.
2. Ask students to list their basic human rights. Use the first starter in the *Student Book*. Do animals have any of the same rights?

3. Use the second starter in the *Student Book*.

4. Show students other pictures of the ways animals are used, for example: for work (guide dogs, police dogs, sheep dogs), for entertainment, for medical or cosmetic testing. Ask them to respond to each picture. Take votes on whether each use should be allowed or not.

Activity guidance

- Refer students to Units 1.6, 2.3 and 2.6 to help with Activity **1** in the *Student Book*. They could explain their ideas by writing one or two paragraphs.

- After students have prepared their arguments for Activity **2** in the *Student Book*, organize a class debate. Ask students who agree with the statement to stand on one side of the room, those who disagree on the other side. Those who cannot decide should stand in the middle and move to one side or the other when they have something in the debate to persuade them.

- The assembly in Activity **3** of the *Student Book* will be a class effort. The whole class could agree on what they want to cover and then split into small groups to plan and put together various components, which could involve speaking parts and visual displays of various types.

Ideas for plenaries

1. Ask students to share the paragraphs they wrote for Activity **1** in the *Student Book*.

2. Ask students to write their own response to what they have learned in this lesson, using the sentence starters: 'Buddhist views on animal rights are... My views on animal rights are...'.

3. Ask students to work in pairs to make a word search based on Buddhist views on animal rights. The easiest way might be for clues to be statements with missing words. They can then swap and solve another pair's word search.

4. Ask students to consider the following: 'When walking a narrow path, pure and earnest bhikkhus will never so much as tread on the growing grass beside the path. How can a bhikkhu, who hopes to be a deliverer of others, himself be living on the flesh of other sentient beings?' (Surangama Sutra). What do they think this passage teaches about respect for living things?

Further class and homework activities

1. Encourage students to do some research to find out about the beliefs and practices of members of the Jain faith who take precautions against destroying the tiniest forms of life, even accidentally. How does this compare to Buddhist practice?

2. 5.4 Animal Rights Interactive Activity on the *Buddhism Kerboodle*.

3. Further suggestions on page 92 of this book.

5.5 Can Non-Violence Really Work?

The unit in brief

This unit explores Buddhist beliefs and views on the use of violence. It gives examples of Buddhists actively promoting peace, as well as examples of Buddhist practice that seem to embrace violence. It also gives students the opportunity to reflect on a world without violence.

Key ideas

- Buddhism teaches the way of peace and non-violence
- In order to practise Right Action, Buddhists would avoid doing a job that involves using force or violence
- However, many martial arts, as a method of self-defence, are associated with Buddhism
- Some Buddhist monks killed themselves in protest against the Vietnam War
- Other Buddhists, including the Nipponzan-Myohoji order, actively promote peace

Skills practised

- Thinking: reflecting on the use of violence and whether non-violence can work
- Literacy: writing a speech, play or story regarding non-violence
- Interpretation: creating a poster explaining Buddhist teaching on non-violence
- Enquiry: finding out about individuals and groups promoting non-violence
- Communication: giving a presentation on individuals or groups promoting non-violence
- Reflection: considering how Buddhist beliefs on non-violence can be followed by ordinary people

Resources

- 5.5 Conflict Film Clip: Tom discusses how the principle of non-violence affects his life
- 5.5 Film Worksheet: students assess their understanding of the case study film clips by linking ideas to the *Student Book*
- 5.5 Views on Violence Interactive Activity: students assess their knowledge about Buddhist views on violence
- 5.5 Lesson Player: a ready-to-go presentation with built-in resources and teacher notes
- 5 Image Gallery: a useful gallery of photos and illustrations from the chapter
- 5.5 Self-assessment Sheet: students evaluate their learning against the lesson objectives

Ideas for starters

1. Use the starter in the *Student Book*. Students could start by listing the benefits of a world without violence, or suggesting ideas to be listed on the board.

2. Revist the quotation from the Dhammapada on page 70 of the *Student Book* and ask students what they think it means. Draw out that it does not refer only to killing, but to all violence. What does that encompass?

3. Give students examples of current conflicts in the world and ask them to suggest non-violent ways to solve the conflict. Even if they do not know details of specific conflicts, they should be able to suggest negotiation and looking for common causes.

4. Ask students if they can think of any situations in which the use of force would be acceptable.

Activity guidance

- Allow students to discuss the questions in Activity **1** in the *Student Book* before writing. They could do this in small groups or as a class.

- For Activity **3** in the *Student Book*, students could start by researching the Nobel Peace Prize, the work of Amnesty International or individuals such as Martin Luther King or Mahatma Gandhi. This is a good opportunity to compare the attitudes of different faith leaders to non-violence.

Ideas for plenaries

1. Use the Reflection from the *Student Book*. You could draw out what students understand about Buddhist beliefs and/or what their own views are.

2. Ask students to present their speeches, plays or stories from Activity **1** in the *Student Book* to the rest of the class.

3. Ask students to give their presentations from Activity **3** in the *Student Book* either to the class or in small groups.

Further class and homework activities

1. Ask students to look at the Peace One Day campaign website. They should decide whether or not they agree with this organization's work and be prepared to explain why.

2. Ask students to produce a short written answer or diagram that compares Buddhist views about violence/non-violence with these of another faith system, for example, Quakerism. This could work well as a homework activity.

3. You could use 5.5 Film Worksheet on the *Buddhism Kerboodle* at the end of the lesson to help students consolidate various views on non-violence.

4. 5.5 Views on Violence Interactive Activity on the *Buddhism Kerboodle*.

5. Further suggestions on page 92 of this book.

5.6 Thich Nhat Hanh: Man of Peace

The unit in brief

This unit introduces the life and work of the Zen master Thich Nhat Hanh. It explores the way in which he has engaged in social action and worked for peace. It also gives students the opportunity to consider whether faith is the best motivation to help others.

Key ideas

- Thich Nhat Hanh is a Zen master known as a peace and human rights activist
- He founded a movement called Engaged Buddhism, which gives people practical help in recovering from conflict
- He has led many peace rallies and delegations
- His teachings appeal to a wide range of people

Skills practised

- Interpretation: explaining the meaning of 'peace' and 'social action'
- Enquiry: investigating the life and work of Thich Nhat Hanh
- Analysis: discussing whether the world would be a better place if more people engaged in social action
- Teamwork: designing a project to help the local community
- Literacy: writing text for a presentation on the life and work of Thich Nhat Hanh
- Reflection: considering what motivates people to help others

Resources

- 5.6 Teachings Audio Clip: a reading of some of Thich Nhat Hanh's teachings
- 5.6 Engaged Buddhism Worksheet: students outline a project for followers of Engaged Buddhism
- 5.6 Thich Nhat Hanh Interactive Activity: students complete sentences about the life and work of Thich Nhat Hanh
- 5.6 Lesson Player: a ready-to-go presentation with built-in resources and teacher notes
- 5 Image Gallery: a useful gallery of photos and illustrations from the chapter
- 5.6 Self-assessment Sheet: students evaluate their learning against the lesson objectives

Ideas for starters

1. Use one or both of the starters in the *Student Book*.
2. Ask students to discuss in pairs any times when they have volunteered to help others. Share feedback. Draw out their motives, what they achieved and how they felt after helping.

3. Create a mind-map on the board on what students think the needs of their local community are. Aim to generate four or five strong ideas ready for work on Activity **2** in the *Student Book*.

Activity guidance

- For Activity **1** in the *Student Book*, recap on responses to the second starter in the *Student Book*. Ask students to discuss the questions in the activity in small groups.

- For Activity **2** in the *Student Book*, refer back to the mind-map for the third starter on the opposite page. Small groups could each select and develop one project.

- Students should find a wealth of information for Activity **3** in the *Student Book* and on the Internet, for example at Plum Village's website or buddhanet, as well as in various online newspaper articles.

Ideas for plenaries

1. Use the Reflection from the *Student Book* as the basis for a short discussion.

2. Ask groups to present their proposals for social action in the local community from Activity **2** in the *Student Book*. The class could vote on the best activity and, if possible, put it into action.

3. Select students to give their presentations on the life and work of Thich Nhat Hanh.

Further class and homework activities

1. Students could use 5.6 Engaged Buddhism Worksheet on the *Buddhism Kerboodle* as an alternative way of completing Activity **2** in the Student Book. The worksheet includes a template for their project proposal.

2. Set students the task of researching other people who have promoted peace, for example, Gandhi or Martin Luther King.

3. Ask students to compare Buddhist teachings about peace and conflict with the teachings of the Society of Friends/ Quakers, showing similarities and differences. Some additional research may be required for this task.

4. 5.6 Thich Nhat Hanh Interactive Activity on the *Buddhism Kerboodle*.

5. Further suggestions on page 92 of this book.

Chapter 5 Further Suggestions

These suggestions are addressed directly to students.

5.1 British Buddhists – Who Are They?

1   Create a poster to encourage British Buddhists to stay strong in their faith. **

2   Find out in which areas of Britain Buddhism is most popular. *

3   Take a survey of people in your class or year group about their religious views. Present the results as a bar chart or pie chart, or explain them in one or two paragraphs. **

4   Create the timetable for the meeting of world religious leaders suggested by the Dalai Lama. What rules for the meeting should be agreed on? For example, 'No shouting out'. ***

5.2 Growing Up: The Buddhist Way

1   Find out about people who have fought for equality. For example, you might like to investigate Emmeline Pankhurst, Martin Luther King, Sojourner Truth or Nelson Mandela. Prepare a short presentation on one of them. **

2   Investigate different traditions for rites of passage in Buddhist countries. ***

3   Compare Buddhist teachings and practices on relationships with those of other faiths you have studied. ***

5.3 How Much is Enough?

1   Research a breakdown of what an average British family spends in a month. Keep the categories fairly general. You could start by looking at www.ons.gov.uk: search the section called 'Release calendar' for 'Family Spending, 2012 Edition'. Which items do you think are absolute essentials and which do you think people could do without? **

2   Do you think that if everyone lived by Buddhist principles regarding money the world would be a better place? Remember to consider Right Livelihood as well as using money to help other people. **

3   Write a story with the title: How Much is Enough? *

5.4 Special Feature: Do Animals have Rights?

1   Why do you think that some Buddhists do not object to animal testing for medical research? Write two or three paragraphs to explain your views. **

2   Find out about views on the treatment of animals in other faiths. **

3   Do you think that animals and humans should have equal rights? Be prepared to explain your views. ***

4   Start a scrapbook or collage wall in the classroom about animal rights. You could use cuttings from newspapers and magazines, or download images and take notes from the Internet. *

5.5 Can Non-Violence Really Work?

1   Do some more detailed research on modern conflicts around the world. Choose one. You could collect newspaper cuttings or write your own summary about it. Then suggest some non-violent solutions to the conflict. *

2   Why do you think people use force and violence in situations of conflict? Create a mind-map to show your ideas and be prepared to explain them. **

3   List jobs that a Buddhist would try to avoid doing because of their belief in non-violence. *

5.6 Thich Nhat Hanh: Man of Peace

1   Find out more about the work of the Plum Village community. Make a leaflet explaining what it does. ***

2   If you were given the chance to interview Thich Nhat Hanh, what questions would you ask him? Write ten really good questions. **

3   Do all faiths practise peace? Compare views on peace and war in Buddhism and other faiths you have studied. **

Chapter 5 Assessment

Assessment in the *Student Book*

You will find an assessment task at the end of every chapter that focuses on AT2. In this chapter, the task asks students to plan a weekend series of workshops for lay Buddhists to help them meet the challenges of being a Buddhist in modern Britain.

In the *Student Book* (and on the supporting worksheets), you'll find guidance about levels of assessment that you can use to help your students understand what their work should include. You could ask them to use these criteria for self- or peer-assessment once they've completed the task.

Assessment Task for Chapter 5 (pages **76–77** of the *Buddhism Student Book*)

Objectives

- Identify key aspects of the Buddhist way of life
- Evaluate the importance of learning more about Buddhism
- Show understanding of Buddhism in practice by planning a weekend of workshops for lay Buddhists

Task

Plan a weekend series of workshops for British lay Buddhists. Participants will want to know learn how to live out their Buddhism in a practical way and meet the challenges of life in modern Britain. They will need clear teaching on issues such as relationships, animal rights, how to deal with conflict and how to use their money.

a Plan the main elements of the programme for the workshops, which will be held in the local town hall. Participants will arrive on Friday night after work and leave on Sunday afternoon.

b Prepare a leaflet to advertise the weekend to British Buddhists.

Assessment in *Kerboodle*

On the *Buddhism Kerboodle*, you'll find resources to use when introducing the assessment task to the class.

You can use the *Chapter 5 Assessment Task Presentation* as a front-of-class tool to help your students unpack the assessment criteria, and understand what is expected of them.

Chapter 5 Assessment Worksheets accompany the task, so that once you finish the presentation, your students can easily get started.

Auto-marked tests

The *Buddhism Kerboodle* also contains auto-marked tests for each chapter to help save you time setting questions and marking for AT1. The test for this chapter contains 15 questions and will take most students about half an hour. Test results are automatically stored in the markbook.

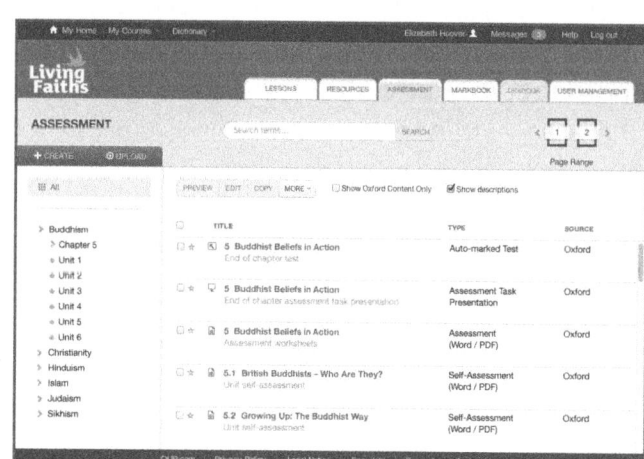

▲ Assessment resources for Chapter 5 on the *Buddhism Kerboodle*

Digital markbook

A markbook and a reporting function complete the *Kerboodle* assessment package, so you can keep all your students' test results and assessment scores in one place. This can include the auto-marked tests as well as pieces of work you or the students have marked by hand.

Glossary

Abhidhamma basket
The deeper, philosophical teachings of the Buddha

Anatta The Buddhist belief that there is no permanent self or 'soul'

Anicca Impermanence in the world; everything changes and nothing lasts forever

Anjali mudda The gesture of putting the hands together in a prayer-like position and bowing the head

Ascetic Someone who lives a life of self-denial, often in order to reach a spiritual goal

BCE Stands for 'before the Common Era', which began roughly 2000 years ago

Bhavacakka Buddhist art that represents the universe symbolically

Bhikkhu Buddhist monk

Bhikkhuni Buddhist nun

Bodhi tree A type of fig tree

Bodhisattva Wise Buddhists who keep coming back to the world after they die to help others

Buddha The Enlightened One; a person who discovers Enlightenment for themself

Buddharupa An image of the Buddha

Canon A collection of sacred writings

CE Stands for 'Common Era', which began roughly 2000 years ago

Craving A constant desire for things and experiences

Dalai Lama The spiritual and political leader of Tibetan Buddhism

Dhamma The teachings of the Buddha

Dhamma Wheel (Dhammacakka) A wheel with eight spokes that is a symbol of Buddhism and represents the Noble Eightfold Path

Dukkha Dissatisfaction or suffering in life

Enlightenment The state of full understanding about the way things are in life

Ethical Living and working by doing the 'right' thing

Five Precepts Practical, ethical guidelines for living a Buddhist life

Four Noble Truths The Buddha's teachings on the nature of suffering: illness, cause, cure exists, cure

Four Sights The four sights that deeply affected Siddattha: an old man, a sick man, a dead body and a holy man

GDP Gross Domestic Product; the total value of all goods and services produced by an economy

GNH Gross National Happiness

Impermanence When something doesn't last and can change

Kamma/karma Actions that are the result of the choices people make

Koan A puzzle-like question that a Zen master asks a novice or trainee

Lama A Tibetan Buddhist teacher or leader

Lay People who follow a faith but are not ordained

Lotus flower A flower that is similar to a water lily and is a symbol of Buddhism

Mahayana The Great Vehicle; one of two main schools of Buddhism

Mandala A sacred design within a circle

Mantra Words to meditate on and focus the mind

Middle Way A life that involves neither great excess and extravagance nor great poverty and deprivation

Multicultural A society that contains several different cultural groups

Multifaith Something that involves a variety of faiths

Neuroscience Studies that focus on the structure and function of the brain and nervous system

Nibbana/Nirvana 'Blowing out' the fires of greed, hatred and ignorance, and the state of perfect peace that follows

Nibbana Day/Nirvana Day Celebrates the Buddha's death and his reaching a final Nibbana; occurs in February

Nipponzan-Myohoji A school of Mahayana Buddhism that developed in Japan

Noble Eightfold Path
The Buddha's Middle Way: Right Understanding, Right Attitude, Right Speech, Right Action, Right Livelihood, Right Effort, Right Mindfulness, Right Contemplation

Ordained Those who, in Buddhism, train to be and are made into monks and nuns

Pali The language of many early Buddhist scriptures; an ancient language originating in northern India

PhD A high-level academic qualification

Prostration A movement where the body is laid flat on the ground, with the face down, before getting up again

Puja Buddhist worship

Pure Land School of Buddhism that believes in reaching Enlightenment through meditation on Amida Buddha

Retreat A withdrawal from everyday life for a period of quiet thoughtfulness, usually in a monastery

Samana A holy man who lives a life of poverty

Samsara The endless cycle of birth, death and rebirth, with all its suffering

Sangha The community of Buddhist believers

Sanskrit The ancient sacred language of India

Secular Without religious reference; non-religious

Siddattha or Siddhartha
The personal name of the Buddha

Stupa A conical object that represents the Buddha's holy mind

Sutta/sutra Text; the word of the Buddha

Sutta basket The most well-known teachings of the Buddha

Theist A person who believes in the existence of a god or gods

Theravada The Way of the Elders; one of two main schools of Buddhism

Three Refuges/Three Jewels
The three most precious things in Buddhism: the Buddha, the dhamma, the Sangha

Three Signs of Being Anicca, dukkha, anatta

Tibetan Buddhism A school of Mahayana Buddhism that developed in Tibet

Tipitaka The Three Baskets; the three collections of writings that make up the Pali Canon

Upsaka A member of the lay Buddhist community

Vinaya basket The teachings of the Buddha that make up the set of rules for monastic life

Wesak A festival on the full moon of the month Wesak (in May or June) to celebrate the birth, Enlightenment and death of the Buddha

Zazen Seated meditation

Zen Buddhism 'Zen' comes from the Sanskrit word meaning 'meditation' or 'concentration'; a school of Mahayana Buddhism that developed in China and Japan

Great Clarendon Street, Oxford, OX2 6DP, United Kingdom

Oxford University Press is a department of the University of Oxford.
It furthers the University's objective of excellence in research,
scholarship, and education by publishing worldwide. Oxford is a
registered trade mark of Oxford University Press in the UK and in
certain other countries

British Library Cataloguing in Publication Data
Data available

978-0-19-915061 8

10 9 8 7 6 5 4 3 2

Paper used in the production of this book is a natural, recyclable product
made from wood grown in sustainable forests.
The manufacturing process conforms to the environmental regulations
of the country of origin.

Printed by Ashford Print and Publishing Services, Gosport

Acknowledgements

The publishers would like to thank the following for permissions to use
their photographs:

Cover: Corbis

From the author, Mark Constance: I would like to thank the students
of Balcarras School who, with their questions, answers, humour and
thoughtfulness, have made teaching RE the best job in the school.

OUP wishes to thank the Aldam and Harvey families, as well as
the community of the temple Wat Santiwongsaram and Phra Aod
Boonyoung in particular, for agreeing to take part in the case study films
and to be photographed for this title.

Although we have made every effort to trace and contact all copyright
holders before publication this has not been possible in all cases. If
notified, the publisher will rectify any errors or omissions at the earliest
opportunity.

Links to third party websites are provided by Oxford in good faith and
for information only. Oxford disclaims any responsibility for
the materials contained in any third party website referenced in
this work.